CW01021701

The True and Living God

Kim Hawtrey

How today's false gods rob us of real life

MATTHIAS MEDIA

Copyright © 1998 Kim Hawtrey
St Matthias Press Ltd ACN 067 558 365

PO Box 225, Kingsford NSW Australia 2032
Telephone: (02) 9663 1478   Facsimile: (02) 9662 4289
International: +61-2-9663 1478   Facsimile: +61-2-9662 4289
E-mail: matmedia@ozemail.com.au
web site: http://www.gospelnet.com.au/matmedia

St Matthias Press (UK)
PO Box 665, London SW20 8RU, England
Telephone: (0181) 942 0880   Facsimile: (0181) 942 0990
E-mail: MattMedia@compuserve.com

ISBN 1 876326 09 3

Cover design and typesetting
by Joy Lankshear Design Pty Ltd.

Printed in Australia.

Contents

Acknowledgements

The writing of this book was generously supported by a grant from the Australian Research Theology foundation, whose assistance is gratefully acknowledged.

Sincere appreciation is also due to Tony Payne who provided very helpful comments and suggestions on an earlier draft. Any residual errors, nevertheless, remain my responsibility entirely.

I also wish to thank the individual supporters and churches who have worked in partnership with IMPACT Evangelism over the years; you have provided invaluable opportunities and encouragement in the ongoing work of gospelling, for which I am deeply grateful to God.

K.H.

Preamble

A year or so ago, I learned a lesson from a river that I will never forget. It was late summer, and a bunch of us were booked in for an adventure weekend of white-water kayaking. During the four hour drive to the river country, I remember feeling pretty confident about what lay ahead. After all, it was not my first time kayaking; in fact as a boy I had successfully passed a canoeing certificate at camp, and over the years had been on a number of similar trips to this one.

I told myself it would all be smooth going. I was going to deal with the river on my terms.

That was before I found out about the rain. Just before our arrival, it poured with rain on the high tablelands which feed that valley with runoff, so that by the time we arrived, the river was really flowing. And I mean flowing.

All of us capsized a number of times, we lost shoes and sunglasses (not to mention our dignity), and at one point I really thought I was going to drown.

I had gone there expecting to deal with the river on my terms, but by the time I left, I was dealing with the river on its terms.

God is like that river. Just when you start to think he is tame, you discover his awesome side. Mind you, it is an easy mistake to make. According to the Bible, all of us, without exception, like to assume we can deal with God on our own terms.

Big mistake. It simply doesn't pay to be complacent about where we stand with him. I have learnt that we have to deal with God on *his* terms, and his terms alone. Any other way simply won't work. Like the river, God is not someone we can be casual about. He has an awesome nature. He cannot be tamed.

Is that how God is seen today? To be frank, the answer is no.

As I hope to show in the following chapters, we live instead in a society that follows the gospel according to *House and Garden*, that looks for hope in the latest Hollywood movie. There are numerous pointers to the fact that across our quiet dormitory suburbs, God has been basically replaced by counterfeit goals. How do I know? Because I also struggle with these issues daily. I'm speaking from personal experience.

Instead of the awesome God of the Bible who occupies the throne of heaven, our culture has domesticated him to an absent (or at the very most, manageable) deity, placing him at the back of the queue. In his place, we substitute less important pursuits. This seduction by the secondary is the subject of this book.

My aim is to direct attention back to the true and living God, Jesus Christ, who is infinitely more wonderful than anyone or anything else I know.

And whether I succeed in this task depends as much on you, the reader. So please take a deep breath, keep an open mind, and read on…

KIM HAWTREY
(khawtrey@pnc.com.au)
Sydney
November 1998

God and Our Goals

When I was fifteen years old, I owned a road racing push bike. It was superb. It had ten speed gears, shiny red paint and a really smooth ride. I peddled it everywhere, and to me it was the best thing since sliced bread. I would not have swapped it for anything.

Except an electric guitar. At the age of seventeen I traded in my beloved bike for my first rock guitar. In the face of limited finances, I had to make a tough choice. It wasn't easy–giving up the bike that meant so much to me– but I was motivated by gaining an even better thing. That guitar was a beauty. It was black, loud and had a 'wah wah' lever that must have driven the neighbours mad. Nothing in the world could have induced me to part with it.

Except an engagement ring for my fiancé. At the age of twenty one, still basically broke, I sold my precious guitar to raise the cash I needed for a diamond ring. It was a tough thing to do–selling the guitar, that is–but it was for a greater love and I knew it was worth it. (You will be pleased to know that I have never since traded in the engagement ring on something else!)

In many and varied situations like those I have just described, we have to make choices. Choices between competing loyalties. Sometimes the nature of these choices is fairly trivial, like whether we have chicken or beef for dinner tonight. At other times, they are somewhat more significant, and reveal something deeper about us, such as a decision to stay home for an important family birthday party rather than go out with friends to a concert we rather wanted to see. Indeed, often the toughest decisions are when we are forced to choose between two legitimate options, neither one wrong in itself. This is when we really show our true colours.

Life seems to have a way of regularly involving this kind of process, where we have to choose between two or more valid alternatives that are admirable in their own right but cannot both be given first priority. It is then that we must decide what ranks as most important, and each time this happens there is a kind of 'moment of truth', revealing what (or whom) we value *the most*. In my simple example above, when the chips were down, I valued my future marriage relationship more than the bike or guitar. It was not that these other things in themselves were 'bad' or 'wrong', but that there was a greater love that made its claim on me. Imagine what kind of message it would have sent my future wife if the guitar had mattered more to me than she did! Our real life choices, therefore, often demonstrate what we truly love.

This principle applies all the way up, ultimately, to the greatest question of all: God and our relationship with him. What we chase after most in life—what we ultimately aim for above all else—is an issue that matters a great deal to God. And there is a point at which our choices reveal what we truly think about God, because sooner or later we find ourselves deciding which we will make number one: God, or the many good things that go to make up this mesmerizing world of ours.

Everybody worships something

Many people today claim they believe in God, but the question is: what do our unspoken choices and behaviours say? Woody Allen once quipped that "you can't ride two horses with one behind"! His point was that, when all is said and done, we have only one life to live and cannot ultimately do justice to two competing dreams. The Bible puts it this way: we cannot serve two masters. Either we will hate the one and love the other, or be devoted to one and despise the other (Matthew 6:24). This core principle is put to the test by anything in life that has the potential to command our ultimate loyalty in place of God.

To see this in proper perspective is the subject of this book. And a good starting point for getting a handle on things is to realise that everybody—including you and I—*worships* something (or someone).

Right now, you might be thinking: "Hold on a moment…did he just say worship?…what has worship got to do with anything?" And it is understandable some might react this way, thinking 'worship' is not relevant to them. Perhaps they are 'not the religious type'; perhaps they think that worship is something that only occurs in an organized church service. What has 'worship' got to do with the ordinary choices of the average person?

The short answer is: quite a bit actually. In the Bible, worship is a much broader idea than just what happens in church on Sunday: it refers to the whole box and dice of what (or who) we *serve* and pursue in everyday life, because this is the true measure of where our hearts really pay homage. In particular, Scripture says we can mistakenly **"worship and serve created things rather than the Creator"** (Romans 1:25). In other words, those who do not

worship God (and who therefore probably regard themselves as non-religious) are in actual fact worshippers without even knowing it. It is just that they don't explicitly label
the things that they serve 'god'.

Think of it this way. Whatever we ultimately serve, day
in and day out—from our career through to our possessions
through to our homespun philosophy—can be seen as the
object of our 'worship'. We can even be caught up in serving ourselves or living in homage to another human being.
Worship simply means to exalt or enthrone something (or
someone) in our ordinary thinking and practice such that,
when the chips are down and we have to make a tough
choice, it commands our higher allegiance. It may be
conscious or unconscious, but at the end of the day, we
march to the beat of its drum.

It is therefore too narrow to think of worship simply as
something that 'religious' people do in a church building
on Sunday morning. And this raises a vital question: *Who or
what am I serving?*

Our aspirations matter to God

A question like that above deserves an answer, for one
important reason. And it is this: God is deeply interested in
what we, as human beings, are devoted to—in our 'heart of
hearts' if you like. Christianity poses the question of what I
value first in my life, over and above all else. It says there
is a vital link between what I am seeking after most of all—
what I am pursuing most vigorously—and how I stand with
God. Our whole lives, in effect, are a manifestation of what
we think about God.

Here's the crunch: we live in a society that is apparently
devoted to everything **BUT** God. In our world, God is not

allowed to be God. The sad fact is that the world is full of people pursuing the things God has made, or the gifts God has given, or the self God has created, rather than God himself.

At first, this might be difficult to see because so often the pursuits we all run after are not 'bad' in themselves–things like work, family, home, environment, politics, clothes, individuality, learning, television, money. In their proper place, these are all good gifts and have a legitimate contribution to life's overall tapestry. But the trouble is, they have a perverse way of getting put centre-stage, with God being constantly denied or shunted offstage into the wings. This is a subtle and insidious thing we all do, according to the Bible, and which we may not even be aware of. It is not that we actively campaign against God; it's just that we ignore him. We simply follow a course in life that *our own* intuition plans for us.

As we grow up and life begins to open out to us, with all its possibilities, everything seems natural to us and we get swept along by the current. We plot our course through life, and develop our own little batch of 'must-haves', our personal recipe for who we want to be and what we want to do. 'Never lose sight of the big picture' a clever advertisement tells us, and it is tapping into precisely this part of us–our *aspirations*. Although we may not voice them very often, these goals are very important to us. As singer songwriter Paul Simon has put it, "no-one gives their dreams away too lightly, they hold them tightly" *(Jonah)*.

God addresses this part of us, our 'aspirational' self. This will come as a surprise to many, because popular thinking today has reduced religion to only a limited sphere of relevance, namely our 'moral self'.

Yet the Bible often talks about aspirations, especially in terms of where our *hope* lies. The New Testament repeatedly emphasizes how critical this question is, speaking of those who are without God as being "without hope" (Ephesians 2:12) and often using the idea of hope to capture the place where we locate our deepest longings for the future (Romans 8:25). Hope is seen in terms of our inspiration for living (Colossians 1:4-5). Our deepest hopes matter to God—not just our morality as in popular perception—and to have 'faith' somehow involves all our aims and values for living.

Our highest aspiration should be to know God. The Bible makes this a constant theme, urging us to "seek first his kingdom and his righteousness" (Matthew 6:33). The writer of the Psalms says that our focus in life should be on our Maker, saying "my eyes are fixed on you, O sovereign Lord" (Psalm 141:8). What we hunger and thirst for most is a vitally important question, according to the Bible, revolving around whether it is God we thirst for (Psalm 42:2, Matthew 5:6) or someone or something else we might pursue in competition with him (Matthew 6:24).

The core issue

In these pages I will be posing one simple question: What does it mean for God to be king in our lives? We will look at this in three parts.

The first section is diagnostic. It identifies the symptoms of when we are not allowing God to have his rightful place in our lives; when we are allowing 'the world' to be our worship. We need to get to the heart of things, and expose today's tinpot 'God-substitutes' for what they are, for as the Bible puts it "a man is a slave to whatever has mastered him"

(2 Peter 2:19). These God-substitutes can be anything in life that we love more than God himself: prestige, success, popularity, money, power, pets, homemaking, fame, security, sport, comfort, career, education, promotion, marriage, better car, travel, privacy, superannuation, talent, fashion, food, beauty, tolerance, drink, movies, control, intellect, success, autonomy, and so on. Many of these rivals to God are not 'bad' or 'evil' at face value; in fact, they are often good things in their proper place. But good things can become the very agents of rebellion against God when they are ranked higher than him. Each of the items listed is capable of holding our heart hostage, of dominating our life at the expense of God and keeping us in a kind of spiritual death. Section one illustrates what this might look like using several common examples.

Part II presents the one true alternative worthy of our devotion: Jesus. These chapters give a straightforward portrait from the Bible of the living God as he really is, in the person of Jesus Christ, so that that we might be struck by the sharp contrast between the false suburban 'gods' and the real God. We will see that the message of Christianity is more revolutionary than simply a mainstream lifestyle with a bit of morality tacked on the end.

The third and final section explains how to turn from 'idols' to serve the true and living God. An encounter with God through his Son Jesus Christ turns our lives upside down, inverting our aspirations and changing our hopes forever. It not only gives a new hope for the future; it has implications for the present in terms of changed priorities and new relationships. Instead of serving self, we have a fresh sense of purpose that involves loving God and loving others. A strange revolution in our thinking begins to take place. Turning to Christ necessarily involves subverting the world's false values.

Sometimes, the change of direction can be very public. New Zealand rugby player Michael Jones was widely expected to be picked to represent his country in the World Cup in South Africa, yet in an announcement that shocked everyone, he made himself unavailable for selection, saying (rightly or wrongly), "My faith means I do not play on Sundays"; a while later, leading Australian jockey Darren Beadman announced his unexpected early retirement and sent shockwaves through the racing fraternity, stating that he wanted to become a minister of the gospel; in New Testament times, a corrupt tax-collector named Zaccheus decided to repay his ill-gotten gains four times over to those he had exploited (Luke 19:8).

What would motivate such strange behaviour? We're about to find out.

PART 1

The self-serve society

CHAPTER 1

The Genesis Blueprint

In the movie *City Slickers*, a film about some regular middle-class guys in mid-life crisis, there is an important point in the story when the three friends are out on the range, driving the cattle (and rediscovering the 'cowboy inside'!). The whole experience causes them to think deeply about what life means. Billy Crystal asks the others: "Do you want to know what the secret of life is?".

"It's this", he says, answering his own question and holding up a single index finger. "It's One Thing. You have that One Thing and everything else is secondary."

Crystal doesn't go on to tell us what the One Thing might be, but he is right as far as he goes. There *is* one thing that makes sense of life, and the Bible says the one thing is the Lord God.

Unscrambling the egg

In Genesis 1 and 2, the opening chapters of the Bible, we read that God created the world. He made everything good, and gave many wonderful gifts for humanity to enjoy. In particular, he made us, like a potter fashions clay (Isaiah 64:8). God brought us into existence, and we each owe our being to him. We belong to him, and so we are to worship him as creator and God. This teaching is so foundational, it is virtually never defended in the Bible; it is simply taken as given, requiring no defence. As the clay has no right to question the potter (Romans 9:20), mankind should not consider any other course than to exclusively worship and serve the living God.

Equally significant is the order of things God established from the start. At the creation, human beings are placed in a set of *ordered relationships*. When God creates the world, everything is in its rightful place: God is the sovereign ruler of all creation, including men and women; in turn, mankind (under God) rules over the plants and animals. It is a picture where each of the elements of creation is living in ordered harmony with each other and in tune with God. In particular, animals and the environment are subject to mankind, and in turn mankind is subject to God (Genesis 2:16-20).

These two original 'orders' of creation are like two pillars, established by God, on which everything else is built:

- the first pillar says that God should rule over mankind, as sole rightful king; this means we are created to worship our Creator, and nothing must be allowed to intervene or reverse this relationship (for example, we should not worship created things, including any human being, even ourselves);

- the second pillar says that mankind should preside over the rest of the creation, under the kingship of God (Genesis 1:28); here, men and women are said to be created in the 'image' of God, involving a sort of vice-regency role in caring for the creation as God's representatives. A key implication is that it would be wrong for us to do anything that upsets this divinely ordained ordering–for example, mankind must not allow the lower created things (objects, plants or animals) to become master, to effectively rule the human ruler. Created things must not be allowed to take over our lives, for that would effectively amount to a reversal of the original ordering. Humanity, in other words, must not worship anything else in place of God.

This God-given scheme, established at the creation of the world, is very special. It is the vital clue to who we are, and where we fit. Comedian Robin Williams, who was recently voted Number One in a poll that ranked the world's greatest comedians, sometimes has a wonderful way of getting us to think about what it is means to be a human being (remember his performance in *Dead Poet's Society*). Like in his 1994 movie *Being Human*, which ran under this trailer:

From the dawn of time man has struggled for just four things:
Food. Safety. Someone to love.
And a pair of shoes that fit.

The film tells five short tales of a man named Hector who finds himself in different time zones, ranging from way back in the Bronze Age right through to a modern metropolis. It is an odyssey stretching across thousands of years and yet told through a single character, the running theme being mankind's need to make sense out of the world and put things in some kind of order.

At one level, the Bible is just like that movie: it too is an epic story starting at the creation of the world and moving down through the ages. Here too, a key character in the saga is Man, who is depicted as a creature with an ordained place in the order of things. Unlike the movie, however, the Bible gives us the answer to the puzzle: *everything hinges on worshipping the Creator and not worshipping creation.*

This is the key to unscrambling the egg. Think about it for a moment. As even existentialist thinker Jean Paul Sartre put it, there is something about "the glory, the horror and the boredom of being human" that cries out for an answer beyond ourselves. And here is the answer. It is not simply the fact that we human beings are wonderfully made, although this is true–the human eye can distinguish six million colours; at birth, a baby's brain contains 100 billion neurons, roughly as many nerve cells as there are stars in the Milky Way. Nor is it only our superior intelligence (albeit sometimes exaggerated: *Popular Mechanics* magazine once predicted that by the year 2000, we would all have cybernetic butlers who would fly us to work in a helicopter!). It is something more.

Ultimately, it is the fact we are made in the image of God with the capacity for personal relationship with the Creator, that makes us humans distinctive. It gives us a special place in creation. And the potential to mess up. It has been said that what makes us different from animals is the ability to lie. We human beings can exercise our wills independently; we can make plans for the future that may be good or bad. We have some degree of moral awareness, knowing that there is such a thing as right and wrong. We can decide between one course of action and another, evaluating which is the more worthwhile. We can give–and withhold–our allegiance. And we can fall into the trap of making ourselves subservient to mere created things.

What a glorious and yet serious business life is. It is glorious because the original plan of God is perfect and he allows us to play a unique role in his grand scheme. But it is serious, because tampering with the ordained order of relationships has very dangerous consequences. This should make us stop and think.

The perfect plan

The blueprint for life found in the Bible presents us with a pattern of relationships and priorities that is set by God from before the beginning of time. It requires us to relate to God and the world in a certain manner, and there is a sense in which God calls us to be 'narrow-minded' in adopting his blueprint to the exclusion of alternatives.

This is made explicit in a famous image from the New Testament, when Jesus speaks of two roads, one wide, one narrow:

> *Enter through the narrow gate. For wide is the gate and broad is the road that leads to destruction, and many enter through it (Matthew 7:13).*

What's more, Jesus continues, "small is the gate and narrow the road that leads to life, and only a few find it". One implication is that following the crowd in life may put us out of step with God. Think about it for a moment. If 'many' travel the broad road, and this road leads to 'destruction', then there is the distinct likelihood that the aspirations of the majority in any given generation are unlikely to be true. The philosophy of 'Joe six-pack' and 'Jill regular', of Mr and Mrs Average, is likely in the sight of God to be faulty in outlook and essence, and to lead ulti- mately to rejection by him.

If we come to the conclusion that normality is usually heresy, it goes without saying that we are to radically dissent from normality. We ought to treat the popular plan for living, with its corresponding complacency about God, with a profound suspicion. Even the decadent Oscar Wilde said: "I hate it when people agree with me, because then I know I must certainly be wrong".

It follows that the biblical blueprint contains within it a sense of world-denial. While Christianity is world affirming at a very significant level (and so we should be careful not to fall into the error of monastic withdrawal or a gnostic view of flesh as 'evil'), there is at the same time a sense in which Christianity calls upon us to be world-denying by rejecting the authority of the world. Jesus said that "if anyone would come after me, he must deny himself and take up his cross and follow me" (Matthew 16:24). And in 1 John 2:17 we read bluntly, "do not love the world or anything in the world". As someone once said, religion at its very heart is a way of 'denying the authority of the rest of the world'.

The first step is to recognize that the biblical blueprint begins and ends with the rightful place of God as God. This is what is at stake in the very first of the Ten Commandments, where God says:

You shall have no other gods before me (Exodus 20:3).

This commandment is the foundation on which all the others rest. It has in view a *relationship*, because there is assumed a prior commitment by God to us. The Bible is full of heartfelt relational language as it describes God and us. Martin Luther put it this way in his *Preface to the Old Testament*: the laws of God "must and ought to be measured by faith and love". At the heart of the law of God, in other words, lies the love and fidelity of God. This is the context behind the commandment to have no other gods but the true God: namely, a relationship of trust and commitment with his creatures. God's objective is always to restore and maintain a love-relationship with us, a so-called 'covenant' friendship.

The bottom line is this: God is fully committed to us, but he does not stand in any queues. We are to be absolutely single-minded in our devotion to God and his kingdom, to be in essence a *prime-passion person*. There is to be no greater dream in our heart than to know God. A believer loves God more than life itself (Matthew 16:25).

Such a person does not ration their attention to God; they lavish it. They do not give God a lukewarm, 'left-handed' welcome into their lives but a fully devoted, right-handed one. Their heart is really in it, their whole heart. As J.C. Ryle wrote, such a person "sees only one thing"—cares for one thing, lives for one thing, is swallowed up in one thing—and that One Thing is "to please God" (*Practical Religion,* 1878). Their highest aspiration is to know God. Jesus made the demands of God stark in Luke 14:

> *Any of you who does not give up everything he has cannot be my disciple (verse 33).*

As singer Celine Dion croons, such love "doesn't think twice". Whether winter or summer, whether comfortable or distressed, whether liked or disliked, whether respected or ridiculed, it matters little to such people. Their one goal is to honour God, day in and day out. Such a person has no price, and will never sell out.

Seeking first his kingdom

So the prime-passion person will put God number one, and put everything else at number two. But it is important to realise that this applies *even to the good things in life.* Even the most wholesome and proper parts of creation—such as family, home, or work—will need to be put in their place if they are looming as rivals to God.

Surveys show that a majority of people claim they 'believe in God', but this can be put to the test by how each person lives. A. W. Tozer puts it this way:

> *Let (the average man) be forced into making a choice between God and money, between God and men, between God and personal ambition, between God and human love, and God will take second place every time.*

These other things will consistently be exalted above God. The true state of affairs will be revealed by the rankings we make day after day. It is often this type of choice—between the everyday and the eternal—that represents the sharpest moment of truth. It is on the edge of the envelope, at the margin, that we discover where our true loyalty lies. This type of choice is a constant theme in the Bible, where it is presented from a number of angles. Here's a couple:

- *seeking first the kingdom*: this is the theme of the Sermon on the Mount. Jesus says, "Do not worry about your life, what you will eat or drink; or about your body, what you will wear" (Matthew 6:25). These have their place (our heavenly Father knows we need them), but they are not the most important things to pursue. We should instead "seek first his kingdom and his righteousness" (Matthew 6:33). Here, the priority principle—of choosing to pursue the best thing before the other good things in life—is clearly taught by Jesus.

- *forsaking all to gain heaven*: our relating to God implies a willingness to forsake everything else. The kingdom of

God, said Jesus, is like a treasure hidden in a field. When a man found it, he hid it again, and then in his joy went and sold all that he had and bought that field (Matthew 13:44). In other words, he saw as of little value all the other affections and attachments that were previously so dear to him, in order to know God. What he gave up was not 'evil'; it was just less valuable.

The common denominator in these biblical excerpts is the idea that to 'believe' in God, to really know him, I will make all else subsidiary and put him first in my life. I am meant to normalize my life around him.

The biblical blueprint does not just push the envelope of our worldview, it rips it. Putting God in his rightful place involves 'forsaking all else', and implies a massive reversal of our aspirations in life. Christianity requires more than just a spiritual renaissance; it requires a complete revolution. It is summed up in the famous words of the historic *Westminster Confession*: "The chief end of man is to glorify God and to enjoy him forever".

The jealous God

The exclusive blueprint of the Bible has a flipside: it means that God is jealous for his name and willing to defend his rightful place as Lord.

There is a 'jealousy' which God exercises. At first, this sounds unattractive. By and large, jealousy has something of a bad name in our society, perhaps because it conjures up in our minds those trashy midday TV soap operas with their shallow characters and superficial storylines. You know the sort, the ones whose plots revolve around naked envy: "Will Jake finally get his revenge on Trent for beating him to the top job at MegaCorp? Find out today on

Baywatch Place!" We tend to see jealousy as a vice rather than a virtue, and many of us perhaps are not used to speaking of God as 'jealous'.

Yet there is a better side to jealousy. Shakespeare knew that one of the recipes for great drama is jealousy. A good example is *A Winters Tale*, which tells the story of Leontes, King of Sicilia. Leontes believes that his wife is carrying the child of his best friend, and finds himself in the grip of jealousy. The result is an intense and moving saga that explores the subject of betrayal, and reminds us that there is a time and a place when jealousy is both right and proper (see for example Proverbs 6:32-35).

In the right sense, God himself is jealous. Jealousy is right and proper for God when we let something or someone else rival his rightful place in our lives. As John Calvin wrote, "God is provoked to jealousy as often as we substitute our own inventions in place of him" *(Institutes of Christian Religion,* Book II, chapter 8). It is an essential part of his character to be jealous. In fact, his jealousy is not unlike that of a husband for his beloved.

In the biblical book of Hosea, for instance, God is aroused to jealousy because "there is no acknowledgment of God in the land" (Hosea 4:1). In other words, Israel was simply ignoring God. Like a husband who is entitled to be jealous as his wife plays the harlot, God is entitled to be jealous when people do not worship him as God. This is the jealousy of God, in the admirable sense of keeping faith. The jealousy of God is constructive, not destructive. It is protective–a justified rivalry towards those who would destroy or distort what he stands for. God's jealousy is a positive type of jealousy, like the jealousy a spouse should feel if their marriage is invaded by another.

When God calls himself jealous, it is because he is unable to bear any other loyalty that shares our allegiance. This theme keeps popping up again and again through the Bible.

God's jealousy is directly linked to his holiness (Joshua 24:19), and when violated provokes his righteous anger (Deuteronomy 6:15). We read that God will "direct his jealous anger" against us if we cheat on him (Ezekiel 23:25), and that he avenges his honour (Nahum 1:2). In the New Testament it is the same: God's jealousy is real, and we risk inflaming it if we turn our backs on him (1 Corinthians 10:22).

This type of jealousy ultimately defends an underlying relationship from attack, either from without or within. It springs from love, not from hate. Such jealousy is a virtue, and it is the flip-side of love. If there is no jealousy evident when relationships come under threat, then it is a sure sign there was little genuine love in the first place.

Believing in the blueprint

It's often said, as Billy Crystal did, that if you get the One Thing right in life, everything else will fall into place. Some say the One Thing is money: "Make enough money and everything will follow", as one of the corporate lawyers said in *Ally McBeal*. Others say: "No, it's your family; nothing's more important than family". Yet the Bible says: "Seek first the kingdom of God". This is true wisdom.

The Genesis Blueprint desperately needs to be rediscovered. As we will see in the next chapter, ours is a society which allows the created order to be overturned. At the level of our individual lives, we are repeatedly turning God's plan upside down—and back to front—by marching to the drum of created things rather than our Creator, and by failing to worship God as God.

While there is a sense in which we have lost God amid the wonders of his world, yet we can find him again, amid the wonders of his Word, if we are willing to listen to his voice in the Scriptures. In an age when some 200 million e-mail messages crisscross the planet every day, are you and I still willing to hear the voice of God above the din, and rediscover the way things were meant to be?

Selling Out

In the newspaper recently there was the sad story of the funeral of a man. All funerals are sad in their own way, but this one had an added element of pathos. All his life, according to the article in the paper, the man had dreamed of winning big on the races, and shortly before he died, his dream had come true. At the funeral, a giant television screen was set up behind the coffin so his friends and family could relive his moment of 'triumph'. "We replayed the race because that was his ultimate goal", relatives were quoted as saying. The object of his worship was there, but he was gone.

Tearing up the instructions

It's an example of our goals gone wrong. It all started way back, when human beings decided to tear up God's original blueprint and began distorting the ordered relationships God had put in place.

The story is told in Genesis chapter 3. God had commanded Adam and Eve not to eat of the fruit of the tree of the knowledge of good and evil, and they openly disobeyed. All of a sudden, both sides of the divinely ordained order for life were turned upside down, and it has been the same with every person since.

The first ordering we humans have overturned is the

worship of God as God. Since the day Adam and Eve ate the forbidden 'fruit', humanity no longer submits to the Creator. The clearly defined boundary of the creature-Creator relationship, found in the command to Adam not to eat of the tree (Genesis 2:17), has been violated. The creature was rebelling against the Creator, out of a human aspiration to be 'like God'. Effectively, the man and woman were trying to usurp God's kingship, to occupy the throne that rightfully belongs only to God.

The second aspect, the other side of the same coin, is that the rest of creation no longer submits to mankind. The serpent (an animal) directs the human, rather than *vice versa* (Genesis 3:4). And the 'curses' that are pronounced by God as punishment for sin show that the harmonious set of relationships instituted by God at creation are broken: the soil no longer yields its bounty easily, forcing the man to work with toil and sweat (3:17), and the woman now has greatly increased pain in childbirth (3:16). The planned vice-regency of humanity over the rest of creation has now become vexed and fraught with trouble. In some sense, we even become like mere beasts ourselves (2 Peter 2:12). In short, sin has spoiled the original Genesis blueprint.

Human beings now allow themselves to be ruled by created things. The New Testament sums up the situation this way:

> *They exchanged the truth about God for a lie, and worshipped and served created things rather than the Creator…(Romans 1:25).*

When you and I worship and serve created things rather than the Creator, we are simultaneously violating the two orderings from the original blueprint of God: we are failing to worship our Creator alone, and we are allowing mere created things to have mastery over us.

The Bible says that living this way is to "exchange the truth about God for a lie". And we all do it. Although "since the creation of the world" God's "eternal power and divine nature" have been clearly evident (Romans 1:20), mankind has "neither glorified God nor given thanks to him". So, says the Bible, we are all caught up in the sin of Adam and Eve; we each worship worldly things in our lives, and we each commit the mistake of elevating created things above God. In effect, using the analogy of a ring, we focus on the setting and neglect the diamond.

Engrossed in the world

Trying to live this way—under the spell of people or things—is a universal character trait, because we are all tainted with sin. Effectively, everyone "lives for themselves" rather than for God (2 Corinthians 5:15). The Bible says that in doing so, our thinking becomes "futile" and our "foolish hearts are darkened" (Romans 1:21). We absolutise the contingent things in life. We take the secondary things of life, and try to make them primary.

The objects of our distraction can range from house remodelling, to fitness, to fame, to personal independence, to money, to Elvis Presley. When we accept the lie that God is not God, we become lovers of the world (1 John 2:15) and the Bible condemns such a choice in no uncertain terms:

> *You adulterous people, don't you know that friendship with the world is hatred towards God? Anyone who chooses to be a friend of the world becomes an enemy of God (James 4:4).*

Worldliness, in other words, is the antithesis of godliness.

And it stems from where our heart is: if our treasure is in the world, there will our heart be also (Matthew 6:21). Instead of loving the Lord God with all our heart (Matthew 22:37), the Scriptures say that our natural tendency is for our hearts to be far from him (Mark 7:6) and to instead treasure worldly things: status, prestige, power, autonomy, and the list goes on. We have gone down the slippery slope of worldliness.

There is a seductive side to this phenomenon. The world can fool us into thinking we are gaining greater liberty, the allure of a greater freedom, when in reality we are being ensnared (Proverbs 5:22). Although in the final analysis love for the things of this world leads to a no-man's land, we are blinded to this fact by their attractions. An old saying puts it this way: though they offer nothing upstairs, boy oh boy, do they have a fantastic stairway! Even appetites as simple as food and drink can enslave us. Like in the TV ad that says, 'obey your thirst'. Or the T-shirt announcing that 'BEER IS LIFE'. Or when Esau sold his birthright for a bowl of stew (Genesis 25:34). When we worship at the altar of our passions and pleasures (Titus 3:3), when we allow the flotsam and jetsam of this passing world to bury our lifestyle, we are no longer free as God intended. As Frederica Mathewes wrote recently, "We want to believe that following our hearts' desires will lead us to Candyland" (*Current Thoughts and Trends, September 1996*).

In the face of all this, the New Testament warnings are crystal clear:

> *For everything in the world—the cravings of sinful man,*
> *the lust of his eyes, and the boasting of what he has and*
> *does—comes not from the Father but from the world*
> *(1 John 2:16).*

Such earthly masters are slippery customers. They can make us begin to believe the words of W. S. Gilbert, who famously said that 'life is a pudding of plums' and that all we need do is stick in our thumb and pull out something to our liking. Our devotion to them is often subconscious, a beneath-the-surface obsession or assumption that may lie buried deep in our wills. Half the time we are not even aware we have them. Our society brainwashes us into such a frame of mind that our values become invisible to us, like the accent we learn to speak with. In its most basic form, the worldly 'altar' we 'worship' at is simply our daily approach to life. As Leslie Newbiggin has put it, our 'world-view' is what we think about the world when we are not really thinking! Even telling ourselves that we are easy-going and tolerant, not religious, and that we have no point of view other than to take each day as it comes, is *itself* a form of worship.

One of the temptations presented to Jesus by Satan in the wilderness was that of gaining the world:

> *The devil led him up to a high place and showed him*
> *in an instant all the kingdoms of the world. And he said*
> *to him, "I will give you all their authority and splendour,*
> *for it has been given to me, and I can give it to anyone*
> *I want to. So if you worship me, it will all be yours"*
> *(Luke 4:5-7).*

There is a connection between seeking after the world and worshipping Satan, who is after all merely a creature and not God. Jesus replies:

> *It is written "Worship the Lord your God and serve him*
> *only" (verse 8).*

We are to serve God only, for he alone is truly worthy of

our worship and devotion. And somehow this is connected with resisting the temptation to pursue the world first and foremost, for this is one of the lies propagated by the evil one. Elsewhere, on a similar tack, Jesus asks his hearers, "What good will it be for a man if he gains the whole world, yet forfeits his soul?" (Matthew 16:26).

So the issue of worldly pursuit is a very serious one, having the potential to cost us our soul. Unlike the true God, worldly 'gods' can be seen and touched–that is part of their allure. By contrast, the living God is invisible (Colossians 1:15). Such false 'gods' trivialise and diminish the authentic God, but we love them because they fit our desire to be self-absorbed and self-referencing.

At the base of it all is self-worship. Without God, we are "lovers of self" (2 Timothy 3:2). Our unspoken creed becomes the 'I' statement so prevalent in our society today. For example, an advertising campaign for a major credit card showed various hip and successful people stating beliefs like: 'It's my life, I can spend it any way I like' and 'I'm going to spend more time doing the things I want to do'. These are the lies we tell ourselves to rationalize our rejection of God's claim on our lives

The good as the enemy of the best

Clearly, then, even *the good can become the enemy of the best.* This is because although valid in their place, good things can be so attractive as to seduce us away from God. Jesus told a parable to illustrate this in Luke 8.

A farmer went out to sow his seed. As he was sowing, some fell on the path, some on rocky ground, some among thorns, and some on good soil. The seed that fell among thorns, Jesus says, stands for those who hear the word of God, but as they go on their way they are choked by life's riches, worries and pleasures, like a plant that is choked by weeds, and so they never grow in God and mature spiritually.

As we go with the flow, following the great Australian dream and setting our own goals, this is exactly what can happen. We sell out the promises of God, enticed by the lights and dazzle of the world. But the Bible says this about us:

There is a way that seems right to a man,
but in the end it leads to death (Proverbs 14:12).

The problem is that invariably the tail begins to wag the dog. Instead of working to live, we start living for work. Instead of controlling the TV, we begin allowing it to control us. Instead of money being our servant, it becomes our master. And so on.

When God is no longer treated as God, then secondary things get elevated to a status way beyond their true importance. It is the spiritual equivalent of putting a $2000 stereo in a $200 car: we allow life to get all out of proportion. Pretty soon, we are putting great effort and resources into things that matter little (such as living in a B-grade suburb instead of a C-grade one), and at the same time neglecting the things that matter a lot (like knowing God instead of being a stranger to him). Consequently, today our suburbs are full of people fussing over what the Bible regards as the flotsam and jetsam of life, while at the same time being unconcerned about the really important (eternal) things. It's as if we have put the proverbial red pen through God's list of rankings and priorities, and re-set the list to suit ourselves. At the end of the day, we are guilty of wresting the agenda out of God's hands and placing it squarely in our own. This is the essence of what the Bible calls sin, and it produces a society that is self-absorbed and in denial of God.

It's a false shadow of how life is meant to be. A futile quest. For one thing, our homemade substitutes for God inevitably fail to satisfy, like chewing gum that loses its flavour. After ten or fifteen years of chasing the dream, there is still something missing. So we go out and try more of the same: a better job, a new pair of shoes, double the fun, a bigger house, greater public recognition. We try to make bearable the hollowness of our souls without God by a strategy of constant distraction. And if we keep racing after more things and more experiences, then perhaps we won't have time to notice that it's not working. But it is like running in a dream, when you run and run and run without moving from the same spot.

Ask yourself this question: what will be your epitaph? 'He worked for IBM.' 'She had an inground pool.' 'He had a great CD collection.' These are nice things in their season, but they hardly constitute a reason for living. C. S. Lewis once said that our basic human yearnings constitute a news bulletin from a country we have not yet visited, the echo of a tune we have not yet heard, the scent of a flower we long to find. When we close our ears to that bulletin, we do not experience life as it was truly meant be experienced.

Yet that is not the half of it. The world has a way of stealing the most important thing from us so that we never realise it has gone: our standing before God himself. The adverse implications of our misdirected priorities, in other words, go well beyond just a vague subjective sense of dissatisfaction, however disquieting that may be. There is an objective price to pay as well, and it is huge.

Under God's judgment

The Bible warns against being polluted by the world for good reason (James 1:27). *Firstly*, as noted above, worship of the world does not deliver. It fails on an existential level, because it does not satisfy who we were created to be. False absolutes are skim milk masquerading as cream. The Bible recognizes this subjective element, in the words of Ecclesiastes: "Whoever loves money never has money enough; whoever loves wealth is never satisfied with his income" (5:10). The world's 'gods', in the words of folk duo Indigo Girls, 'kiss you like a lover, then they sting you like a viper'. They promise much but end up leaving us striving for more, like hamsters on a circular treadmill. Instead of freedom, love of the world represents a very real form of slavery.

Secondly, and more importantly, love of the world and our corresponding failure to treat God as God, puts us under divine judgment.

This is objective and real. When our aspirations are focussed on the visible world and not on God, we have no hope of salvation; our destiny is destruction (Philippians 3:19). We are hopelessly devoted to the wrong thing. We are under the judgment of the living God.

These days, it has become somewhat unfashionable to talk in such a way. But to that idea, let me say that it is very dangerous to shrug God off so lightly. Jesus warned that it is quite possible to become ensnared by the "anxieties of life", and then suddenly find that the day of judgment closes in on you "unexpectedly like a trap" (Luke 21:34).

Jesus also said: "Whoever tries to keep his life will lose it, and whoever loses his life will preserve it" (Luke 17:33). He drew a contrast between two groups of people. In one group are those whose focus is on earthly matters, who have paid scant attention to God, only to find that when the day of judgment comes they are not ready:

> *Just as it was in the days of Noah, so also will it be in the days of the Son of Man. People were eating, drinking, marrying and being given in marriage up to the day Noah entered the ark. Then the flood came and destroyed them all (Luke 17:26-27).*

They had been engrossed in the things of the world, 'getting on with their lives', and had not paid attention to their relationship with God. Jesus illustrates again:

> *It was the same in the days of Lot. People were eating and drinking, buying and selling, planting and building. But the day Lot left Sodom, fire and sulphur rained down from heaven and destroyed them all (verses 28-29).*

Whoever tries to "keep his life"—to locate his hope and purpose principally in this earthly life—will ultimately lose it. The judgment of God is true and tangible. Contrary to the trend of post-modernist relativism, life is not an open playground of self pursuit; it is not consequence-free.

On the day of judgment our worldly gods will not be able to save us. Although not 'idols' in the strict sense of a statue, they are similar at this point: like idols, they are dead. Our earthly 'gods' can do nothing for us—they cannot save us, and they cannot love us. Isaiah highlights this, when he points out how ridiculous it is for living human beings to be captivated by, and place their reliance on, anything of man's own making (Isaiah 44:15-17). The New Testament echoes this, saying "we know that an idol is nothing at all" (1 Corinthians 8:4). There can be no doubt that we fully deserve God's judgment. Loving the world and ignoring him amounts to a challenge to his position as God, because our worldly vanity and desire for unchallenged self-determination come from our basic sinful desire to usurp God's position.

Ultimately, this is the real reason people have a problem with Christianity. Deep down, it is not that church is old-fashioned (we happily join golf clubs with more traditionalism), nor that sermons are boring (compared with our weekly sojourn in the supermarket?!), nor that science has disproved the Bible (it hasn't), but rather that in our heart of hearts we reject the right of the living God to run our lives—in every department. This is the real explanation for why we are cold to our Creator, and why we prefer to pursue created things.

The essence of our love for false gods is an attempt to figure out *for ourselves* what we want and need, rather than letting God define and meet our needs. The prophet Jeremiah summed up the double-edged nature of it:

> *They have forsaken me,*
> *the spring of living water,*
> *and have dug their own cisterns,*
> *broken cisterns that cannot hold water (Jeremiah 2:13).*

At the heart of it, we are trying to disengage from God because we think we know better than him. But our own plans will not, in the final analysis, 'hold water'—as we will see in the next chapter.

Modern Rivals to God

What does it look like in practice when God is no longer allowed to be God? When the good things in life are permitted to crowd him out? This chapter looks at what some of the symptoms might be in our lives, when we are allowing the good to be the enemy of the best. They are presented simply as symptoms that can possibly indicate the underlying spiritual problem of unbelief: of loving the things in creation more than the Creator, of rejecting God's claim to be king in our lives.

We have seen in the previous chapter that what we "run after" in life is the issue (Matthew 6:32). But often it is difficult to recognize it in ourselves, and we may need someone else to point it out for us, perhaps by listing a few indicators. Gradually, we can begin to recognize the tell-tale signs that we are being dominated by a sense of self, not by a sense of God. We see it when our identity as a professional, or as a rich westerner, or as a supporter of our football team, or as a resident of our upmarket suburb, or as a father, or as a standard-bearer of good taste, or as a champion of human rights, or as the life of the party, is instantly felt, but any identification with God is remote or zero. If my sense of 'who I am' is located in such things and not in God, then it will show itself in the dedicated thinking, planning and sense of vision I give them, ahead of God.

What types of worldly loves can ensnare us? It can be a tangible object, such as money and possessions, but it need not be. We can be greedy or obsessive about a whole host of intangible things as well, from fame and fortune right through to privacy and good housekeeping. Whether tangible or not, all our "desires and greed" are called "idols" by the New Testament, in Colossians 3:5 and Ephesians 5:5.

All of a sudden, it becomes clear that a wide variety of things can play 'false god' in my life. I can be a workaholic. I can be obsessed with trading up to a better neighbourhood. I can be a dedicated follower of fashion. My favourite football team can command the best of my time and energy. Equally, traditional values such as high society manners, or a dedication to family, can potentially occupy the place of 'god' in my life. We can be "lovers of money" (2 Timothy 3:2) or of "pleasure" (3:4). It can be a human philosophy, or a personal lifestyle; it can be an icon or an ordinary everyday thing. Or a view of the world that presently holds us captive.

Such worldly loves fight for first place in our lives. They soon form the basis for our 'ego-system'. Such 'sacred cows' become so entrenched after a while that they turn into just another part of the suburban syndrome. In short, when I allow these to get in the way of full devotion to the true and living God of the Bible (with all my heart, soul, mind and strength), I am worshiping the creature, not the Creator.

We can think in terms of several different groups:

1. *Materialism:* examples of this first group include money, house, boat, car, clothes, comforts, appliances, food, technology and so on.

2. *Relationships:* family, spouse, parents, children, friends, mates, boss, customer, pop star, city and country, form examples of how particular people or groups of people can potentially occupy first place on the throne of our hearts instead of God.

3. *Personal cravings:* instead of listening to the voice of God, we can listen to the voice of security, comfort, success, autonomy, entertainment, convenience, visibility, self-fulfillment, talents, beauty, intelligence, pleasure, pride, alcohol, winning, spectacle, prestige, learning, accomplishments, power, popularity, sport, reason, the need to be in control, designer labels, and the like.

4. *Worldview:* a non-Christian ideology may hold us captive, such as individualism, feminism, racism, astrology, Marxism, Freudianism, Darwinism, post-modernism, or moralism.

In the sections that follow, some of the most important of these 'God-substitutes' will be put under the microscope. Some are obvious—at one level you can tell what the pursuits of a society are by simply looking in the weekend newspaper supplements—food, fashion and homes. Some are not so obvious. All, however, can be insidious in their effect.

Love of Money
Live like a king, die like a pauper
In many African tribal societies, the most prized possession is livestock, and in particular the cow. It is a status symbol, and the number of cows owned indicates how successful a person is. And just like westerners with our several cars

and plush homes, the typical African takes great pride in his cow collection. In fact, it is common for an African to keep as many as ten times the number of cattle he really needs, purely for prestige value.

In its own right, money is a not a bad thing. But according to the Bible, the *love* of money is the root of all kinds of evil (1 Timothy 6:10). Materialism is extremely seductive. One reason is simply that it takes us so long to work our way through the whole 'toy shop'. We feel we deserve to experience each and every toy available, and so life becomes a giant exercise in systematically going down the list. We set our heart on experiencing each of the 'feelings': of owning a new car, of owning two cars, of wearing designer label clothes, of wearing the other designer's label, of decorating our home like the one in the magazine, of having the latest piece of technology, of not 'missing out'. And so we move along to the next thing on the list: furniture, kitchen gadgets, travel, foods, bedroom manchester, more clothes, videos, graphite shaft golf clubs, another home improvement, and so on. Sooner or later, we are living to consume rather than consuming to live.

When society buys the myth that God is not supreme, then money and possessions assume prime candidacy as an alternative pursuit. In our western culture, for example, lovely big homes are frequently a suburban icon, with furniture and homeware stores virtually 'sacred sites' that we love to visit. One store advertises 'a whole new experience in home improvement'. American novelist Henry James captured this in his book *Washington Square,* as a young urban couple discuss their aims in life:

> At the end of three or four years we'll move. That's the way you live in this city – to move every three or four years.

Then you always get the last thing... I guess we'll move up little by little; when we get tired of one street we'll go higher. So you see we'll always have a new house; it's a great advantage to have a new house, you get all the latest improvements. They invent everything all over again about every five years, and it's a great thing to keep up with the new things. I always try and keep up with the new things of every kind. Don't you think that's a good motto for a young couple – to keep 'going higher'?

That was written over a hundred years ago, and has anything changed? In the American state of Oregon you can dial up dinner from the American Dream pizza shop. In Virginia, you can hire a limousine from the American Dream limo company. And in Texas, you can buy a home from American Dream Realty. As American historian Richard Hofstadter once said: "It has been our fate as a nation not to have ideologies, but to be one". This basic dream is not restricted to American suburbia: it has been exported around the world, and is dominant in the majority of suburbs from Britain to Australia, from Canada to Japan. All over the world, we are 'California dreamin'.

Aussie cartoonist Michael Leunig put his finger on the power of this agenda in a drawing published recently in the *Sydney Morning Herald*. It showed an ordinary suburban couple sitting on a sofa, looking downhearted as they discuss life after their neighbours have had to sell up and move to another neighbourhood. "Keeping up with Joneses was very stimulating", says the husband, smiling. "Overtaking the Joneses was very exciting", waxes the wife, jauntily. "Watching the Joneses come unstuck was very satisfying", the husband continues. Then there is an awkward pause. They look at each other, their faces forlorn: "Not having the

Joneses is very difficult", laments the husband, sadly. "It is very, VERY difficult", agrees his disappointed wife. Without their materialistic competition with the Joneses, they feel an empty void and a lack of purpose.

The mistake of the materialist is his or her obsession with how well you travel, at the expense of *where you're travelling to.* An advertisement for a leading airline, ironically, puts its finger on the lie behind our consumerism: "Where do you need to be? How will you get there? Does it matter? Yes– the journey is the destination." The journey is the destination, says this philosophy. It is not where you are going in life, but whether you are travelling first or second class that matters, according to the materialism myth.

I need to ask myself honestly: *Am I in the grip of materialism?* Symptoms might be when my relaxation 'release' at the end of each week is to spend or go shopping; when I feel incomplete unless I have the latest state-of-the-art product for home or wardrobe; when I start telling myself that yesterday's whims and luxuries have become today's 'natural' and 'must-have' necessities; when I am so committed to debt repayments that I have no room to manoeuvre and nothing to spare for generosity to others. I might even go to the bathroom during the main TV program so I don't miss the commercials! More seriously, there is the fact that many today know the shopping centre like the back of their hand, but struggle when asked the way to their local church. Are our everyday thoughts and conversations as much about things, as about people or relationships? Can we justify just about anything by telling ourselves: "We've worked hard and deserve it"?

Here's a further set of strong indicators: when I am keener that my kids develop discerning tastes than discerning beliefs; when I 'keep score' in life by ticking off the next item on 'my list' (the decor, landscaping, pool, second car, trip, extension, etc); when I measure my progress down the 'list' against my peers; when I invite friends over for coffee, secretly hoping they will notice my new designer coffee table or expensive sofa.

For many today, all their investments of money, time and energy pay off on *this* side of death. Materialism reflects a lack of eternal perspective. We rush to book our kids into the 'right' schools from the day they are born, to make sure they 'do well' in life, but neglect to instruct them in the things of heaven and God, where their true future lies. This is foolishness, according to the Psalmist:

A man who has riches without understanding is like the beasts that perish (Psalm 49:20).

We are serving money when striving for five-star quality possessions whilst being content with one-star quality religion (or none at all). If so, our lifestyle is based on a lie: the lie of products we don't need, rewards we don't deserve, in-crowds we don't need to belong to, and resources we shouldn't hoard for ourselves. If we live this way–casual about God, serious about possessions–then we are disciples of wealth and enemies of God. The Bible says we cannot serve two masters, God and Money (Matthew 6:24). We think we can have the best of both worlds, but we cannot: we must compromise one or the other. If we give absolute status to our desires for improving house, car, clothes and so on, dedicating ourselves wholeheartedly to achieving them, then it is inevitable we will compromise our relationship with God. We cannot have our cake and eat it too.

The Bible calls upon us to know when enough is enough,

and warns that our love affair with status symbols puts us under the judgment of God. Job says:

> *If I have put my trust in gold, or said to pure gold, "You are my security", if I have rejoiced over my great wealth, the fortune my hands had gained...then these also would be sins to be judged, for I would have been unfaithful to God on high (Job 31:24-28).*

That he ramained faithful to God indicates that he was not preoccupied by his wealth. In many places, the Bible warns of the great danger of trusting in riches or being a lover of money (Proverbs 11:28; I Timothy 6:9-10, 17; Hebrews 13:5).

There is more to life than chasing money, houses, cars, appliances—and juggling our finances to pay for it all. Shopping for happiness never really works; it simply leaves us empty and frustrated inside. Fortunately, because of Jesus there is more to life; much much more.

Captivity to Television

Paying homage to Hollywood

And the people bowed and prayed, to the neon god they'd made. This line, from a famous song by Simon and Garfunkel, captures in a startling way the pervasive influence of electronic media and entertainment (TV, movies, CDs, world wide web) in our lives. The lyrics speak of a society in which interpersonal silence, like a cancer, grows. A society of people disconnected from each other, who in restless dreams walk alone, of songs written that voices never share, of something that had been lost and might never be recaptured.

When God is not recognized as God, human beings look elsewhere for their framework of meaning, and one of the most important worldly sources of such messages is the media. Here's a question: Could you lock your television away in the closet for a month, and not have severe withdrawal symptoms? Figures show that 98 per cent of homes in western nations have a TV, and the average person watches 3-4 hours of television per day, more if we include videos and computer games. By the age of twenty-one, we have spent the equivalent of three full years of our lives in front of the talking box, and watched an estimated 40,000 screen murders. And all of it trying to fathom how Lois Lane can be so blind as not to realise that Superman and Clark Kent are one and the same!

With eyes glued to the screen, the average family home is a place where the TV is on almost all day. A typical viewing pattern looks like this:

7.00am	morning cartoons
11.00am	news and current affairs program
12.00pm	midday soaps or movie
3.00pm	kids' after-school programs
6.00pm	home from work, slump in front of evening news
7.00pm	family eats dinner in front of TV
8.30pm	kids put themselves to bed because the parents are watching evening TV dramas

That is a lot of television watching. Imagine spending four hours a day on any other activity: four hours every day at the pub, or at the supermarket, or at the gym. We would instantly recognize that we were doing that activity to excess, that we had an obsession with it. But not so with our TV viewing. The screen is like a magnet. It has the ability to govern our lifestyle.

One famous example occurred in the early 1980s, when *Dallas* was topping the ratings around the world. The Lap people (who at the same time every year migrate to the south of Lapland for winter) actually delayed their journey for a week in order to find out who shot J.R.!

In New York, it is not enough to watch TV on the small screen–dedicated viewers gather nightly at the corner of Broadway and 68th Street to watch the new Imax Sony 'TV Theatre', a giant screen eight stories high that connects to personal headsets and liquid crystal lenses, giving the illusion of 3D depth.

Recently a local teenager was going on the World Vision 40-hour famine. I put the question to her: What if she could miss out on TV for forty hours instead of food–would she prefer that? A firm 'No' was the reply. She would rather go without food than miss her favourite programs. It's like the old psychiatrist joke. A woman visits a shrink and complains, "Doctor, doctor, my husband thinks he's a television. What can I do?" The psychiatrist replies: "Make an appointment for me to see him tomorrow at four o'clock". She recoils, "What–and miss my favourite program?!"

Trend-watcher Faith Popcorn, in her recent book *Clicking*, describes the compulsive effect of our entertainment obsession in terms of the "ritual of self-reward", which captures the idea that we constantly need a 'fix' at the end of the day or week to compensate for the pressures of modern living.

If we step back for a moment and take a personal 'screen test', what might be some of the warning signals about the dominance of TV on us? Do my conversations too frequently revolve around programs from the night before? Do I set my diary (alter schedules, skip meetings, delay phone calls or neglect relationships) in order to fit around my watching schedule? Am I snapping at others for being interrupted while glued to the set? Is subscribing to Pay TV high on my list of personal plans? Is the TV set allowed to disrupt the family's daily rituals, such as meal-times around the dinner table?

If any of these apply to us, then we are probably under the same spell that captures most of suburbia today. But let's ask ourselves this question: How many pictures in our family photo album show members watching television? Just imagine: "And here's one of little Johnny with his first TV…". Our photo albums never show the countless hours our families spend in front of the box. Why?

The reason is simple. We instinctively know that despite the massive amount of time we devote to it, TV is not ultimately worth much. Television, movies, videos, computer games and the like, are not very significant or spiritually valuable. In fact, these and other forms of entertainment can have severe negative unintended consequences for our worldview, and our knowledge of the meaning of life. They are not just wallpaper in our lives. They are not harmless. They are something more. Ultimately, the issue with TV is not so much how many hours we watch, but whether we submit to its authority by uncritically accepting its worldview.

Firstly, television acts like a preacher. It acts as meaning-maker, presenting a particular worldview to us and shaping our belief. Every night of the week, its loyal suburban congregation dutifully fill their sofa-shaped pews to hear the message. This message does not centre on God, nor does it even recognize he exists most of the time. It is a competitor to God, trafficking in a substitute 'gospel' that implies we can make sense of life without him.

Television gives powerful alternative 'parables'– meaning-laden but man-made stories offering 'wisdom' for living. These shift the emphasis from life or God to lessons on pimples, jeans, fresh breath confidence and lost travellers cheques. Classic examples noted by various commentators over the years are the Parable of the Dirty Ring around the Collar, and the Parable of the Unexpected Phone Call Home to Italy. These sorts of advertisements redefine 'sin' in the marketer's image, as Neil Postman pointed out in his book *Amusing Ourselves to Death*: "Successful advertising uses not what is right with the product, but what is wrong with the buyer/viewer".

Television provides an alternative set of 'faith heroes', role models in sitcoms who win through by believing in themselves. These faith heroes teach us distorted half-truths about family (*The Simpsons, The Mommies),* false goals to aim for (*Mad About You, Beverly Hills 90210),* dysfunctional work and office relationships *(Yes Minister),* and about sexuality gone wrong *(Ellen).* It brings to mind an old saying: 'Let me make the songs of a nation and I care not who makes its laws'. The songs–or the sitcoms–of a nation shape its spiritual direction.

Tragically, through prolonged exposure, the godless content of TV seems normal to us, and we become casual about God, truth and meaning. We become desensitized to evil. A recent survey found that up to 32 violent acts take place during prime time each day, but that 73 per cent of people regard such portrayed violence as just 'harmless entertainment'. It also dulls our ability to hear the message of God, because after a while we can no longer cope with mere words that are not accompanied by pictures. Jacques Ellul has said that as a consequence, "our society is systematically in the process of humiliating the Word, by its preoccupation with images". At the level of our apprehension skills, we become 'fast-food consumers' who make do with a diet of intellectual junk food, with the result that our spiritual nutrition is poor. This 'dumbing-down' leaves us impoverished in our willingness to listen to the voice of God in the Scriptures. As someone once quipped, "the human brain starts working the moment we are born, and never stops until we switch on the TV".

Summed up, the gospel according to television and movies is this: that you are what you own; that getting the best of the other guy is the only game in town; that image matters more than character; that uncommitted sex is normal and acceptable; that lying is sometimes necessary (just don't get caught); that the most important person in the world is you; and that God is not necessary to a fulfilled life. Little wonder Malcom Muggeridge made this judgment: "I see the camera and microphone, far more than nuclear weapons, as the great destructive force of our time. Why? Because they have generated a readiness by the populace to believe lies that is unequalled in history".

Secondly, television steals time. Sometime soon, try the 'next day test' outlined by *The New Yorker* magazine recently: "Last night's movie was two and a half hours of complicated, cross-weaving plots, sometimes gripping and other times funny; violence was always around the corner; overall it was fast and attention-grabbing. But next day it seems like a dream: it gives you almost nothing to remember it by, let alone nourish you." Neon entertainment is our biggest suburban time bandit, and as ancient philosopher Theophrastus said, time is the "most valuable thing a man can spend".

Of course, it is true that TV is 'just a form of relaxation'. It can be terrific. But even in the 'downtime' of my leisure hours, what I fill my mind with can be a way of rejecting God. In the New Testament, we are told to use some discretion when deciding what to focus attention on:

> *Whatever is true, whatever is noble, whatever is right, whatever is pure, whatever is lovely, whatever is admirable – if anything is excellent or praiseworthy – think about such things (Philippians 4:8).*

The great myth of our living room is that it feels like nothing matters there. We can do what we like in our own private universe. We feel unaccountable–a recent government survey found that 82 per cent of people favour allowing adults to view explicit sex and violence in the privacy of their own home–and so we spend night after night in the company of murderers, adulterers, hedonists and people who pay no attention to God.

Without God, we will use something like TV to fill what Pascal termed the 'empty void' in our souls, to escape from real life. The Bible says instead that, "the God of peace will be with you" (Philippians 4:9). Peace does not come from watching the winning Lotto numbers come up on the screen, nor from relinquishing the capacity to think for ourselves, nor from habitual nightly escapes into the make-believe world of TV and movies. These are so much sugar and water in our petrol tank.

Television is not evil by definition, and can be enjoyed like any other aspect of God's creation. Yet, if abused, it can come between us and God. We need to switch on the TV a little less and open the Bible more.

Consecration to Career

When occupation becomes preoccupation

An old French proverb says that 'work is worship'. Could it be that we are in love with our careers to a far greater extent than we are prepared to admit? Most of us work; some of us are driven to hyperwork. An inner compulsion urges the workaholic on, a whispering voice saying that somehow everything hinges on our work. For some, the compulsion is about money—not necessarily wanting to be rich but feeling they 'must' attain a certain standard of living. For others, it is about achievement, about proving themselves—to the boss, to parents, or to colleagues. For still others, it is the fear of failure, or the dream of leaving their mark on the world. Whichever it is, the hard fact is that workaholics are probably almost always driven by a deep personal insecurity.

We work longer hours than we need to. We strain for the next promotion. We often do not get home until the kids are in bed, and see them only on weekends. Our whole life revolves around career goals. These are the symptoms of careerism.

We often joke about our how much we dislike work, but in reality, it is more like a love-hate relationship. When we introduce ourselves to someone at a party, one of the first things we say about ourselves is what we do: "I'm an engineer". Especially for white-collar professionals, our occupation is seen as very, very important in defining who we are.

Work is a good servant, but a poor master. If God is assumed to be out of the picture by our society, then it doesn't take long before we instead become impressed and engrossed in the work of our *own* hands. When our work overwhelms everything else in life, it has become akin to an 'idol'. It takes the place of God, standing on the bridge of our ship but steering us towards the rocks. We need to recognize careerism for what it is—a potential rival to the kingship of God in our lives—and allow God to assume command and navigate our ship back to safe waters.

What are the symptoms of workaholism in my life? When career considerations drive my major decisions and changes, such as marriage breakdown or lifestyle choices. When it affects my close relationships to the point that I require those around me also to be governed by the priorities of my job. When my kids think of me as 'that person who visits the house on weekends'. When career achievements are how I 'keep score' in life, comparing myself to others based on how much money or how many promotions or how many accolades or how big an office so-and-so has. When the trappings of my job keep me fascinated, and I become the guy who talks all through dinner about nothing else but the size of his company car space, or getting the big corner office. When the most precious 'defining moments' in my life are career related—getting a coveted job or promotion—ahead of relational and spiritual milestones. Or perhaps when I see people basically as 'treestumps', obstacles in my path, rather than fellow human beings made in the image of God.

The late English property developer John Redhead worked hard all his life, and made a lot of money. Upon his death recently, he stipulated that his ashes be made into two egg-timers, and be presented to his bank manager and to the taxman. Why? Towards the end of his life, reflecting on the goals to which he had directed his best years, he explained: "One day I suddenly thought I'd worked hard all my life only to hand over most of my cash to the bank and the taxman. When I kick the bucket, I may as well go on working for them."

A committed workaholic is living to work, rather than working to live. Deep down, if the truth be known, we may be using work as an excuse to run–from ourselves, from family, from friends, and ultimately from God. And when we love work too much, it means we value play too little. It is ages since we cooked food over an open camp fire; we can't remember the last time we took in a sunset, played in the rain, left work early to play golf, or went to church by choice.

Why does career or business success become so important to us? We love our work for the sense of validation and legitimacy it gives us. We see it as a way of building up our self-esteem. We each naturally tend to gravitate to where we receive praise and affirmation, and our profession is a prime candidate for this. Yet the Bible has a startling message to us: the most important thing about my career, is that it is not the most important thing.

Loving our career more than we love God will result in the 'winner's curse'. This is when we struggle hard to win in a given contest, only to discover it was the wrong contest. Like Napoleon who successfully invaded Russia but in so doing lost his beloved France, the winner's curse describes what happens when we win one battle but lose the larger war. For instance, when I finally get the promotion I always wanted, but I'm a stranger to my wife; when I have a career, but don't have a relationship with God.

Every year, New York City hosts an annual charity event called the 'Rat Race'. Contestants dressed in full business suits and carrying briefcases run 4 kilometres to the finishing line at Wall Street. In a way, it is a fitting metaphor of daily life for many of us, to which the Bible says that our professional achievements cannot, at the end of the day, deliver the greater satisfaction and salvation that we crave and need. In the book of Ecclesiastes, we are told that in view of the fact of death, all our toil, the sum total of our advancement by human effort, is basically meaningless:

> *For a man may do his work with wisdom, knowledge and skill, and then he must leave all he owns to someone who has not worked for it (Ecclesiastes 2:21).*

The Scriptures urge us to soberly reflect on the fact we are mortal, and to put in proper perspective all our 'anxious striving' and 'labour under the sun':

> *All his days man's work is pain and grief; even at night his mind does not rest. This too is meaningless (Ecclesiastes 2:23).*

Worshipping worldly professional success, in other words, is like 'chasing after the wind'. Work can never feed the soul that is starving for God. To preach otherwise is a lie, as in the infamous motto of Nazi Germany which declared to its citizens *arbach seit frie,* 'work sets you free'. Like their other pet doctrines, that one too was false.

Worse and most seriously of all, being consecrated to our career will come at the expense of our relationship with God. Bill Gates, hard-working founder of Microsoft, recently admitted: "Just in terms of allocation of time resources, religion is not very efficient. There's a lot more I could be doing on a Sunday morning." But as Mark 8:36 warns, "What good is it for a man to gain the whole world, yet forfeit his soul?". This is the most pressing factor of all: dedicated worship of career will cost eternity, because God will judge our ignoring of him. This is the forensic sting in the tale of workaholism, the very real and very dangerous everlasting consequences when we make God play second fiddle. Winning a career but losing our soul is a bad trade. So it is a life-and-death issue: if necessary, we must repudiate our obsession with work if it is preventing us seeking first the kingdom of God.

This means giving work, career and occupation their proper role. And what is this role? The Bible tells us that work is not bad of itself. It was part of God's original blueprint for his creation (Genesis 2:15), being instituted before the Fall. But as a consequence of our sinful nature, not only does work become spoiled and marked by toil (Genesis 3:17), its priority in our lives becomes distorted out of proper proportion. We work too little (Proverbs 10:4), or too much (Jeremiah 17:27), or in the wrong way (Amos 5:11). We need to correct this by being both diligent and yet contented in our daily work. As the writer of Ecclesiastes advises:

> *A man can do nothing better than to eat drink, and find satisfaction in his work (2:24).*

> *To the man or woman who pleases him, God gives wisdom, knowledge and happiness (2:26).*

Instead of being empire-builders, God calls us to be relationship-builders—to seek his face, and to find our significance in him. As we will see in later chapters, in Christ God effectively is saying to us, "I love you too much to simply stand by and watch you work your way into an early grave, sending yourself to hell in the process".

Jeremiah says that when we make our own gods, in reality "they are not gods". They are phony, and this applies no less when we make a 'god' of our career.

Obsession with Sport

When winning is everything

Soccer is a great source of national pride in Brazil. After their national team's loss to France in the 1998 World Cup Final, thousands of Brazilians wept on each other's shoulders on Copacobana Beach, while countless others wandered the streets of Rio, listless and shellshocked.

Like all worldly loves that can potentially take us captive–money, career, beauty–sport is neutral in itself. It only becomes a problem when we make it one, when it comes between us and God. Taken at face value, sport is a healthy thing, a good gift from God that we can enjoy to our benefit. For my own part, I play tennis, ping pong and golf, and enjoy bodysurfing. Yet I am reminded of D. H. Lawrence's remark: "Australians play sport as though their lives depended on it".

For many people today, sport is more than a hobby: it is an obsession. This is especially true of spectator sports, whether a big title fight or Wimbledon or an NBA playoff. An obsession is something that in one sense controls us; we don't control it. When that happens, we are in danger of making the proverbial 'Faustian deal'. According to the story, Faust was promised great power and pleasure, but in return he had to sell his soul. And this is exactly what can happen when we allow sport (and winning) to become our 'everything': we gain the body but lose the soul.

To start with, consider the pride of place given to sport

in the daily media, and the significant language and imagery that is used. I picked up a leading local daily newspaper recently and was stunned to read the leading sports headline: "The feeding of the 50,000" in big bold red lettering. Feeding of the 50,000? Was the Messiah the half-time entertainment? Thereafter followed a blow-by-blow account of a football game that had attracted the devoted crowd, and it struck me how seriously the journalist took it all. The language was reverent and had an almost sacred ring to it: "The Blues rediscovered the pride and intensity that was supposed to have been their hallmark, particularly for a crucial match such as this"; "if there is any historic justice in the game, O'Loughlin's wizardry will serve as the ultimate silent rebuttal"; and the article was littered with words like 'amazing' and 'inspiring'.

Another article started with "The FA Cup runneth over with joy for fans". It spoke of millions of "faithful" viewers as if their greatest dreams had been fulfilled, and treated the Cup itself as a sacred icon: "The priceless cup, made in 1911, is the centrepeice of an international tour by the Cause for Hope Foundation". Elsewhere, a leading footballer appears in billboard advertisements which declare: "Long Live the King!". As I think you will agree, there are very strong pseudo-religious overtones to this way of talking about what is, after all, simply a game of football.

Question: Why is it that top sports stars attract such phenomenal salaries? Even the coaches reflect the value our society places on sport: the highest-paid sports coach today is Rick Pitino who works with the Boston Celtics basketball team. He has a ten-year contract worth over $70 million, and he is not even a player. In press reports, his appointment was described in reverent and worshipful tones: one commentator said Pitino has been "crowned and canonised".

The biggest sport in the world is said to be fishing. In keeping with this, the highest-paid personality on Australian television is not a reporter, not a news anchor, not a serious journalist, but a fishing expert famous for his on-screen routine of kissing fish on the mouth (one wonders what his wife thinks!). Golf is the other fast growth sport, one that is taking over suburbia as the worldwide profile of the game increases. Courses are springing up everywhere and men, women and children alike are teeing off. About one in fifteen people are regular golfers. The newest sports in the world are also making their mark: tandem skydiving, thundercats (inflatable catamarans), paintball (splattering your opponent), jet fighter joy flights (at $10,000 a pop), rap jumping (abseiling over a cliff facing forwards) and kart racing (at speeds of up to 120 km per hour at just one centimetre off the ground). Many a backpacker's life revolves around these thrills.

All of this is fine at one level. But by the same token, there is little doubt that sport—spectator and participatory—attracts a certain kind of dedicated follower. The biggest sports are slavishly followed by millions. In some cities such as Melbourne with its beloved Australian Rules Football, the favourite sport of the population is even jokingly called 'a religion'. Perhaps we might dismiss this as hyperbole, but perhaps there is more than an ounce of truth in it. After all, sport has its 'miracle workers' in names like Tiger Woods, Michael Jordan, Pete Sampras, Mick Doohan and Carl Lewis, seemingly god-like figures who can do things we mere mortals cannot do. And sport has its 'citadels' or temples, sacred sites where the faithful gather and regard the turf as hallowed ground.

How do we explain the fervour of sports crowds, such as those that riot? In most countries, crowds have been known to get more than just a little excited, starting with the 'mexican wave' and—especially in places like Europe and South America—extending to fatal violence and mob rule. In Bucharest recently, for example, spectators at a soccer match between arch rivals Steaua and Dinamo were armed with smoke bombs, coloured flares and soft-drink cans filled with gasoline. By game time, a fire was blazing in the stands and police had to battle two thousand screaming fans to make way for the firefighters. In Brussels, at a European Cup final held at Heysel Stadium, 39 spectators died when fans got out of control. Commenting on such episodes, *Time* magazine said that the heart of the problem is 'identification'—that is, fans somehow locate their core personal identity in their team's fortunes.

Don't get me wrong, I enjoy watching a game as much as the next guy. God gave us the gift of sport and there's nothing intrinsically wrong with enjoying a contest and taking in a game. But at the same time, the pastimes of the world have a way of taking eternal things away, without us realising they're gone. Important things, like meaning for instance. Engrossed in sport, I can soon become chronically 'meaning-challenged'. A letter to the magazine *Christianity Today* recently asked: "How can a culture that finds it perfectly reasonable to pay professional athletes tens of millions of dollars have any grasp of values?". In sport, there can be an underlying value-system that says life is all about winning: winning plays, winning deals, winning smiles. It is a short step from that to the sin bin, and the many stories of conflict, hatred and corruption in dressing rooms and on playing fields everywhere. Some are quite open about it: the motto of the Oklahoma grid-iron team is unabashed: *If you ain't cheatin', you ain't tryin'.* Eventually, we need to stop and ask: what race is it anyhow? what's the prize? which contest really matters in the end?

Sport has gained a kind of deadly mastery over me when it overshadows the role of God in life and causes me to fall into the 'peppercorn rent' syndrome. Let me explain. A peppercorn rent refers to the situation where a tenant pays only the most trivial of sums to a landlord, a laughably low fee, a nominal amount that is way out of all proportion to the true value of the relationship. This is how many people treat God. They 'tip the hat' to him once or twice a year at Christmas or Easter, but essentially neglect their relationship to God week by week. They have lost their sense of what's important, and have allowed something else to take God's place.

Sport, more often than not, is the culprit. It begins to dictate our weekly program and command our primary attention, relegating God to the periphery. This comes to a head on Sundays, when our society consistently chooses sport over church. It may be our own sport or our children's that drags us away, but either way, for many people today it acts as an excuse to opt out of religious involvement. We become absorbed in coaching the Little League, and pretty soon it preoccupies us.

We should not underestimate the allure of being a sports fan. In the words of George Washington, "rare is the man who can resist the highest bidder", and sport makes a very attractive bid for our devotion. Every era in history has had its sideshows, its circus bigtop, its gladiator spectacle, and these have always been seductive in commanding that generation's attention: 'the devil has all the best tunes', according to a common Irish saying.

In our case, the big attraction is sport. It is more important to us to be in the stands than in church. Or to be on the winning team than involved in the kingdom of God. It is a classic example of how even 'beneficial' activities can become addictive, bearing out the ancient maxim: 'nothing to excess'.

God's response to our fatal attraction is tough love. Any addiction that is threatening to our long term well-being cannot be simply handled with kid gloves, and the same applies spiritually: there comes a point where God requires us to make a spiritual choice. No one can serve two masters (Matthew 6:24): either we will be absolutely dedicated to being on the cutting edge of sport, or we will be on the growing edge with God. But we cannot be both.

The words of Scripture show that the things of God must take priority over the physical training of the body:

> *Train yourself to be godly. For physical training is of some value, but godliness has value for all things, holding promise for both the present life and the life to come (1 Timothy 4:8).*

Eric Liddell exemplified this order of priorities, as depicted in the classic film *Chariots of Fire*. Eric was a gifted English runner who competed in the Olympics in 1924, and spoke of feeling 'God's pleasure' when he ran. He likened faith to running in a race–the important thing was to see the race to its end, whatever the cost. And cost him it did. Though a strong favourite to win, he pulled out of the sprint final because it was run on a Sunday, when (rightly or wrongly) he felt duty-bound not to run.

Whatever we may think about competing on Sundays–that is not the point here–we have to admire his devotion to his Lord. He preferred to give up an Olympic gold medal rather than break faith with God. His philosophy was: "If with all your heart you commit yourself to seek God, you will find him" (see 2 Chronicles 15:2).

Infatuation with Beauty

Putting charisma before character

When you walk in the front entrance of a leading department store it hits you. You know what I'm talking about, the pleasant but somewhat overpowering aroma of perfume. It hits you so hard, that comedian Rowen Atkinson was able to get more than a few laughs when his *Mr Bean* character took to the floor, crawling on hands and knees through the makeup section holding a homemade breathing mask over his mouth in the form of a handkerchief, and warning other shoppers away from the 'disaster area'!

Whether you love the smell of perfume, or (like Mr Bean) dread having to brave Cosmetics on your way to Garden Appliances, it raises an intriguing question: Why is the cosmetics counter almost always located where it is? What drives the widespread policy in retailing of giving the beauty department pride of place in our stores? Why do they so often locate it strategically as the flagship of the whole operation?

We don't have to look very hard to find the answer. The beauty myth is alive and well. The desperate, 'idolatrous' longing for looks, personality and charm in our society is everywhere.

Beauty and personal charisma, by themselves, are good gifts from God. But the worship of them is not. And the power of our pride should not be underestimated.

This was illustrated in a true episode a few years ago. Tenants of a tall skyscraper were complaining about the long delays caused by slow elevators, which meant that many busy people were having to stand around in the foyer, bored and impatient, waiting for a lift. Upgrading the elevator system would have been extremely expensive, so the management of that building came up with a clever idea: they installed mirrors in the lobby next to the elevators. Overnight, the complaints stopped and the problem went away. The reason? Patrons of that building now spent the time admiring themselves in the mirrors, and were apparently so absorbed by this pastime that they no longer noticed the delays with lifts.

They had stumbled onto a most basic stimulus to human behaviour: vanity. To be vain is to take excessive pride in one's personality and physique, and down through the ages this has been made into an obsession by one generation after another, even at great expense or discomfort. A century ago, for instance, Paris was swept up in the *Belle Epoque* (1890-1914) during which designers used the 'S' silhouette attained by a corset that forced the chest forward, the waist in and the rear out. In what became known as the 'beautiful period', women subjected themselves to day-long stricture and discomfort for the sake of gaining the look they so desperately desired. On the other side of the world, in China, for centuries the feet of children were bound tightly to prevent growth, simply in the name of a socially sanctioned notion of 'beauty' that admired miniature feet.

Men are not immune from personal vanity either. The fitness and body-building industry is testament to this, along with the explosion of fashion stores for men. Workout videos such as *The Firm* (which promises firm abs in five days) and Dolph Lundgren's *Maximum Potential* (complete with Baywatch setting) are best-sellers, offering 'bodysculpting'. And significantly, such products often talk with neo-spiritual overtones–Lundgren, for instance, quotes Michelangelo: "a beautiful body is the manifestation of a noble spirit".

In its quest for charisma, our society places utmost emphasis on physical beauty. Every day the media present us with images of the 'ideal' body, through TV, magazines and billboards. From the time a little girl gets her first doll, with its hourglass figure and spotless tanned skin, there is an implied pressure to 'look good', and our culture constantly urges people to judge–and be judged–on the basis of appearance. Supermodels adorn magazine covers, because that is what we, the consumers, are eager and willing to buy, reflecting our almost sacred veneration of bodily beauty.

Yet as a billboard recently pointed out, there are only eight women in the world who look like supermodels, and three billion who don't. Not only that, studies have consistently found that $80 jars of 'Swedish exfoliation oils', expensive 'lymphatic draining techniques', so-called 'total body electrolysis rejuvenation' and alleged 'deep probing juices' do little or nothing to slow aging or improve health. Feminist writers have rightly alerted us to the fallacy behind the silicone syndrome of our society. Naomi Wolf, for instance, rightly exposes the tyranny that *The Beauty Myth* has over many women, which causes them to be distracted by things skin deep, as they frantically strive to achieve an impossible ideal.

Yet despite these arguments, our society's devotion to personal appearance remains. Thin still wins, and our teenagers continue to die from eating disorders like anorexia. Television persists in making out that life is one big beauty contest, while the gospel according to *Cleo* and *Cosmopolitan* continues to preach that we *are* how we *look*.

Vanity is both wider and deeper than just our quest for looks: it is also reflected in our general obsession with personal charm as a means of getting others to 'worship' us. Whether through beauty, personality or celebrity, we strive to make ourselves more keenly noticed and to bring others into orbit around us, to be 'charismatic' in the eyes of our friends, colleagues and daily circle. What we ultimately crave is devotion and admiration from others: when society buys the lie that God is a fiction, then we make ourselves 'little gods'. We try to take the place of God, and instinctively want others to revolve around us.

Let's use a little Disneyesque imagination for a moment, and picture life like an orchestra. At the centre stands the Conductor, the chief musician who directs all other musicians and to whom they look for their cue. Surrounding him are the various instruments, all in their turn: violins, cellos, oboes, clarinets, flutes, bassoons and so on. When playing in harmony, they produce a beautiful symphony and each instrument has its own unique part to play.

Now suppose one of the instruments, the assistant violin, decides it is no longer satisfied to play 'second fiddle'. It revolts against the first violin, trying to attract attention and to get the other instruments to admire it. Predictably, others begin to react in the same way –"what's good for the violin is good for me too"–and soon each is trying to outdo the other by preening and strutting so as to be the centre of attention. Where previously there was cooperation, now there is damaging competition. The end result is chaos, a raucous cacophony where nobody 'wins'.

It might be hard to see at first, and even more painful for us to admit, but this pretty much describes you and me at the level of daily life as we vainly attempt to get others—by whatever means—to admire us. There is nothing wrong with charm *per se,* and some of us have more of it than others. But there is something very wrong when we give too much importance to it, when we begin to rely on it and allow it to absorb us. Whether we use looks, fashion, personality or strength, if we are driven by our dream of charming others, it amounts to the same thing: a worship of self.

In keeping with this innate tendency in us all, our society venerates the attractive, the interesting and the famous. From Tom Cruise to Elvis, through to Sharon Stone and Princess Diana, we are fascinated by the so-called 'beautiful people'. David Marshall, in his recent book *Celebrity and Power: Fame in Contemporary Culture,* says such celebrities act as role models for us and have become the glue that holds our lives together, providing a man-made ideal to aim for (a role that rightly belongs to God alone). Deep down, we desire to be like the celebrities, and we imitate them. Lacking true self-esteem from knowing God, and failing to attribute value to the astounding fact that we have *his* attention, we try to compensate by getting human attention.

Without a biblical view of ourselves and of God, we soon get distracted from developing inner character and instead over-emphasize exterior personality, starting with the way we look. No wonder a study published in the *Medical Journal of Australia* found that 98 per cent of female university students want to be slimmer, and this has been traced to feelings of guilt about diet, social insecurity and dissatisfaction with body shape. In other words, there is a connection between our obsession with personality, attractiveness, and wanting to be charming, and our deepest beliefs about who we are and who God is.

Ultimately, if we are caught up in a quest to be the centre of attention, we are rebelling against God. Think back to the orchestra scene: the fiddle was not just competing with fellow instruments, it was in mutiny against the Conductor. There was an attempt to overturn the order of things, to usurp the position of the maestro, and this amounted to a blatant disregard for the authority of the Conductor, an authority that is there for the good of all. This is the greatest idolatry of all: worship of self.

Egocentricity. Conceit. Vanity. Self-absorption. This makes us ugly on the inside, and is called sin.

This is not how God meant things to be. God created us—he is the Master Conductor—and he pronounces every part of his creation to be "very good" (Genesis 1:31). On top of that the Bible says:

> *Your beauty should not come from outward adornment,*
> *such as braided hair and the wearing of gold jewelry and*
> *fine clothes. Instead, it should be that of your inner self,*
> *the unfading beauty of a gentle and quiet spirit, which is*
> *of great worth in God's sight (1 Peter 3:3-4).*

The message of the Bible is that if we truly enthrone God in our lives, we can transcend the false values of our culture; no longer do we need to be dedicated followers of fashion or slaves to the fickle admiration of others. Like a master craftsman of a Stradivarius violin, God fashions us into the likeness of Christ (Romans 8:29). We may not think we are pretty by the world's standards, but God will make us beautiful in character. As someone once said: 'Beautiful young people are an accident of nature; beautiful old people are the product of a life lived in God'.

Worship of Family

The noblest form of atheism

It is not easy to write a section that speaks of the family as an instrument we can use to oppose God. After all, family is literally motherhood and apple pie: everyone knows that families are good and right and proper. So at first, it may be something of a puzzle to see how devotion to our family can be anything but 'Christian'.

Yet it is precisely the noble things in life–especially our families–that are the most likely to present the strongest competition to the very *noblest* thing in life, namely the kingdom of God. This is because the more reputable something is, the nearer it will seem in our minds to a legitimate substitute for knowing the true and living God. This is especially the danger with family life, which is so solid and virtuous that it can easily be mistaken as an approximation to Christianity, and used to deceive ourselves. It is doubly seductive because it captures our heartstrings, making it very difficult to disentangle our strongly-felt loyalty to family from any higher loyalty to God. So we need to open our minds wide and understand what the Bible is saying to us about this crucial area.

In one of the most startling statements in the New Testament, Jesus said this:

*If anyone comes to me and does not hate his father
and mother, his wife and children, his brothers and
sisters—yes, even his own life—he cannot be my disciple
(Luke 14:26).*

What a thing to say! What does he mean? One thing Jesus does *not* mean is this: he is not saying we should all of a sudden start treating our loved ones with contempt. That would clearly be perverse and at odds with other teachings in the Bible about loving our parents, spouse, children and so on. No, something else is being said here.

It is this: according to Jesus, an absolute and overriding devotion to family as our 'everything' can actually keep us out of heaven, if it displaces God from first place in our lives. He is saying that we should put God first, and family second. God expects us to put him above our earthly loved ones.

This was reinforced on another occasion, when a man came to Jesus and said, "Teacher, I will follow you wherever you go" (Matthew 8:19). "But first, let me go and bury my father", said the man. Jesus replied: "Follow me, and let the dead bury their own dead". In Luke's version (Luke 9:61) of the same episode, another similar excuse is given: "Let me say goodbye to my family". Again the same tension is evident, between devotion to family and devotion to God, and the message is that if your family is ultimately more important to you than knowing God, then you do not really know God.

This is where the dedicated suburban family man often goes wrong. He is devoted to his wife and 2.4 kids, their pet dog, their lovely home and the car in the driveway (which needs to be washed every Sunday morning). He is a good dad, works hard for his family, and teaches his kids the 'right' way to live. He spends quality time with the kids and is a great provider, never forgets his wife's birthday and makes sure that when it comes to his family, only the best of everything will do.

There is just one problem, and it is a big one: he is ignoring God. His chosen devotion is noble, and therein lies the most difficult hurdle. Somewhere along the way, he mistakenly picked up the idea that family and fatherhood are somehow a substitute for God and salvation. Unfortunately he is neglecting the best thing, because he is preoccupied with a very good thing. His involvement in church is small or nil, while the best part of his energy each week goes into giving his family 'the very best': earning the overtime money so he can give them those little extras, giving them a top education for their financial future, manicuring the house and lawns so his family will be proud of him.

In a recent survey published by *US News and World Report,* respondents were asked to rank the most important issues in life. 'Family life' was rated number one, chosen by 68 per cent of people, a long way ahead of alternatives such as 'leisure' and 'spiritual life'. The dream of family life as the top way to find happiness is inculcated into us over many years, importantly through pop music. The leading theme in songs on the radio is romantic love and the promise of 'living happily ever after' with our true love. We hear the message over and over again in love songs that the ultimate human experience is to be "up where we belong", when we've "finally found someone" and our "dreams have all come true". Movies and songs try to convince me I will be "on top of the world" when I am "close to you". As social thinker Daniel Miller noted in his recent book *A Theory of Shopping* (Polity Press, 1998), in our secular world we have substituted romantic devotion to a partner for religious devotion to God.

76

This fascination with romance—eventually leading to the dream of the patter of little feet in the cottage with the white picket fence and the cute fireplace—is not high on the agenda of the Bible. In fact, the Bible says if possible we should even consider avoiding romance and family so we are free to concentrate on the things of God. In 1 Corinthians 7:32, Paul writes: "I want you to be free from concern. An unmarried man is concerned about the Lord's affairs—how he can please the Lord. But a married man is concerned about the affairs of this world—how he can please his wife—and his interests are divided". While there is nothing wrong with marriage, the message here is that by putting our obsession with romance and family in perspective, we can be clear in our devotion to the Lord.

One of the most stunning episodes in the Scriptures is God's test of Abraham in Genesis chapter 22. God called Abraham, and said to him: "Take your son, your only son Isaac, whom you love and go to the region of Moriah. Sacrifice him there as a burnt offering on one of the mountains I will tell you about." Early the next morning Abraham got up and saddled his donkey. He took with him two servants and his son Isaac. When he had cut enough wood for the burnt offering, he set out for the place God had told him about. Telling his servants to remain behind, he took the wood, the fire, the knife, and Isaac with him, and as they walked to the place together Isaac became curious and said, "Father?".

Abraham replied, "Yes, my son?"

"The fire and the wood are here", Isaac said, "but where is the lamb for the burnt offering?"

Abraham answered, "God himself will provide the lamb for the burnt offering, my son".

And the two of them went on together. When they reached the place, Abraham built an altar and arranged the wood on it. Then he bound his son Isaac and laid him on the altar, on top of the wood. He reached out his hand and took the knife to slay his son. But at that moment an angel of the Lord called out to him from heaven, "Abraham, Abraham! Do not lay a hand on the boy. Do not do anything to him. Now I know that you fear God, because you have not withheld from me your son, your only son."

Abraham then looked and saw in the nearby thicket a ram caught by its horns. He took the ram and sacrificed it as a burnt offering instead of his son. Then the Lord, through his angel, said: "Because you have done this and have not withheld your son, your only son, I will bless you and make your descendents as numerous as the stars in the sky and as the sand on the seashore...and through your offspring all nations on earth will be blessed, because you have obeyed me".

The force of this story is made even greater when we realise that Abraham had been promised by God that he would be the father of a great nation. Yet here was God telling him to sacrifice his only son, and since Abraham and his wife were already old, this made the prospect of future children decidedly dim.

As we read the story, we are grateful that God is not asking us to give up our own children. Abraham was human just like you and me, and it always deeply moves me to read this account in Genesis; with four children of my own who are each very dear to me, I can feel the agony Abraham must have felt as he struggled to obey God at that moment. Yet what was the point God was making? And does it apply to us? At one level, no. Abraham was a special case, by virtue of his peculiar place in the history of salvation, and we can affirm that God is not commanding you and me to go out and literally sacrifice our kids on an altar. But at another level, God was making a point that *does* apply to us: he wanted to test Abraham, to see where his ultimate loyalty was. The test was to see whether Abraham "feared God". The message is clear: not even our children are more precious than the purposes and claims of God.

This is the startling theological principle in operation here, that we are to love God above all else in life, even our loved ones. We are to place such a high value on God and his kingdom, that we are willing even to put our families second in our decisions and lifestyle, for the sake of putting God first.

Don't get me wrong: family life is wonderful and is one of God's great blessings. But it is not God. It is merely good, not the best. The Lord Jesus modelled this delicate balance perfectly. He was not uncaring of his earthly family, as shown during his crucifixion when—despite his suffering—he still gave thought to his mother Mary by assigning one of his disciples to take care of her after he was gone (John 19:25-27). From that time, the disciple took her into his home. Consistent with this, the Bible teaches us to respect our parents (Exodus 20:12), love our spouse (Ephesians 5:25) and train our children (Ephesians 6:4).

Yet Jesus also showed he had a higher loyalty. When he began his public ministry, his mother and brothers came looking for him and sought to call him away from one of his meetings (Mark 3:31-34). Standing outside the house, they sent someone in to call him. The crowd said, "Your mother and brothers are outside looking for you". Jesus replied: "Who are my mother and my brothers?". Then he looked around at those seated in a circle around him and said: "Here are my mother and my brothers. Whoever does God's will is my brother and my sister" (see also Matthew 12:48-50).

What a seemingly callous thing to say! No doubt his mother and brothers would have been somewhat miffed. Yet Jesus was stating an important truth—that joining the 'family' of God must take precedence over blood ties with our earthly family. The latter last only for this life, while heaven lasts for eternity.

Just in case it still hadn't sunk in, Jesus later states this tension—between the two families—even more bluntly. Speaking in Luke 12:51-53, he says that his mission is not to bring peace but a sword:

> *Do you think I came to bring peace on earth? No, I tell you, but division. From now on there will be five in one family divided against each other, three against two and two against three. They will be divided, father against son and son against father, mother against daughter and daughter against mother, mother-in-law against daughter -in-law and daughter-in-law against mother-in-law.*

There can only be one explanation for these words from Jesus. We are required to give our highest loyalty to the living God ahead of the legitimate, yet ultimately subsidiary, loyalty to our family.

So much for the idols we worship instead of God. They are poor substitutes for the real thing, for the true and living God, who created us and who calls on us to worship him alone. Who is this God? And how can we know him?

PART 2

The One and Only God

CHAPTER 4

The Reality of Jesus

So far our focus has been on the great temptation to love the world, to make it our 'everything', to worship created things instead of the Creator. Now our attention switches. The flip-side of turning away from worldliness is turning to the true and living God. This is how Christian conversion is described in the New Testament:

> ...you turned to God from idols to serve the living and true God, and to wait for his Son from heaven, whom he raised from the dead–Jesus, who rescues us from the coming wrath (1 Thessalonians 1:9-10).

In this part of the book, I want to present the only genuine alternative to love of the world: devotion to Jesus Christ, the true and living God.

Being 'realistic'

Suppose there is a man who does not believe that trains run on Sundays. He sincerely believes this, and is totally convinced in his own mind that on one day of the week, the trains are idle. So he gets into his car to go for a Sunday drive. When he comes to a level crossing, the warning lights are flashing and the bells are clanging, but he does not believe that trains run on Sundays. Despite all the signs, he proceeds to drive across the railway tracks. There is a deafening 'crash!' as the train ploughs straight into his car. The man is killed instantly, but in that split second before impact, as the train is bearing down on him, he has a moment of horrible realisation. It dawns on him how terribly, terribly mistaken he has been. Sincere, yes, but mistaken just the same.

If you and I are to turn from worldliness to believe in God, it is on the basis that God is actually real and living. At first, however, it may seem 'unrealistic' to contemplate a relationship with God. This reflects the fact that, these days, most people's notion of God is vague and uncertain. Notions of God have become opinionated, with the common view being that as long as we're sincere, any view of God is valid as long as it doesn't harm others. Yet Christianity declares that God is in fact *real*, and that the truth about him is very *specific*.

This is important. Suppose there is a man who does not believe anything in particular about God. This man does not agree with the claim that Jesus is the Son of God, that he rose from the dead, that he is alive today and that he will return when we least expect it, as judge of the whole world. He is very sincere in his belief, and feels that nobody needs to believe Christianity if they choose not to, and that following Jesus Christ is a matter of personal opinion. Despite all the churches and preachers, he marches to his own beat, and regards himself as a practical minded person who prefers to live in the 'real' world. So he gets on with life in his own way, believing the motto 'to thine own self be true' and assuming that each person's opinions about God are valid, and that at the end of the day we won't have to explain ourselves to anybody.

Then all of a sudden, he has a heart attack and dies, and finds himself standing before the judgment seat of almighty God, who sentences him to an eternity of separation in a place called hell. And for a split second, before being taken away, he has that terrible moment when the realisation dawns that—like the man who didn't believe trains run on Sundays—he was wrong. And not just wrong. He was sincerely, seriously and eternally, wrong.

The reality of eternity

You may have seen a documentary about a man called Arthur Stace, who is famous for writing the word ETERNITY in chalk on footpaths around the streets of Sydney during the 1930s though to the 1950s. Legend has it that in 1932 he visited a church where the preacher was talking about eternity, and the preacher told his hearers, "The Bible says there is only one eternity, and Jesus is in charge of it". And then, turning aside from his notes for a moment, the speaker remarked, "How I wish that one word—eternity—were written across the streets of our city for all to see!". Apparently, Arthur Stace took it literally, and for the next 37 years wrote his simple one-word sidewalk sermon everywhere he went. In all, it is estimated he wrote the word ETERNITY half a million times!

I guess the question Arthur Stace was constantly putting before those who saw his chalking was this: where will you spend eternity? It is a good question. After all, as someone has said, 'The living are just the dead on vacation'. We would be foolish not to pay attention to our death, and what comes after, because we will have to face it eventually. Eternity is not the right thing to be wrong about. Yet it never ceases to amaze me how casual most people are about their eternity.

Eternity is real because God is eternal. The Bible says "from everlasting to everlasting you are God" (Psalm 90:2) and "the Lord is the everlasting God" (Isaiah 40:28). His kingdom is never-ending (Psalm 145:13) and his rule permanent (Daniel 7:27). Further, the friendship that God offers to his followers—to us when we become Christian—is everlasting (Jeremiah 32:40), while the judgment on those who resist God is likewise unending (Jude 6). Both heaven and hell, in other words, last forever.

The reality of God and eternity, when taken seriously, changes everything. All of a sudden, it is realistic to be concerned about spiritual matters, and unrealistic to be an atheist. No longer can we realistically live just for today, for this world only. And no longer can we worship and serve created things instead of the eternal Creator.

The reality of judgment day

When the apostle Paul arrived in Athens he made this very point (Acts 17). As he walked around the city and looked at their objects of worship (their 'idols'), he noticed an alter with this remarkable inscription: TO AN UNKNOWN GOD. So he stood up and told them about this God they did not know, calling on them to turn from serving idols to the true and living God:

> *The God who made the world and everything in it is the Lord of heaven and earth and does not live in temples built by hands. And he is not served by human hands, as if he needed anything, because he himself gives all men life and breath and everything else (Acts 17:24-25).*

Once we realise that the God of eternity is real, we should

stop worshipping the creature and instead worship the everlasting Lord. Paul puts it this way:

Therefore, since we are God's offspring, we should not think that the divine being is like gold or silver or stone— an image made by man's design and skill (Acts 17:29).

In other words, we should put aside our obsession with transitory things that will pass away, and live in the light of eternity.

So there is more to life than what we can see and touch, and more to the future than just this earth. But eternity is such a vast concept, we can struggle to come to grips with it. So God gives us his specific blueprint for the future, a very precise plan which ties everything down and concentrates the mind. Paul continues:

God has set a day when he will judge the world with justice by the man he has appointed. He has given proof of this to all men by raising him from the dead (Acts 17:31).

Judgment day will be the climax of history, the culmination of all earthly life. It is the one appointment we all face with our Maker, and this forms the user's guide to eternity that we find in the Bible. It is saying that all things find their true purpose and conclusion on that day, when we will all stand before the judgment seat of God.

The Bible says many things about the judgment of God. The wicked will not stand in the face of it (Psalm 1:5) and it will be their own fault, for they will have brought God's judgment down upon themselves (Romans 2:5). For those outside Christ, it will be a fearful prospect (Hebrews 10:27) but those who are 'in Christ' can have confidence on the day of judgment (1 John 4:17). All men and women without exception will face the judgment seat of God (2 Corinthians 5:10) and his judgment will be true and just (Revelation 16:7).

This is breakthrough information. At present, you may live as if you can manufacture your own 'meaning' for daily living, and this will show itself in preoccupation with the worldly things described in chapter 3. But unless God's assessment of your life is involved, it is simply a fable of your own making. That is where judgment day is so critical to our understanding of reality: this single event is the one that will make a proper assessment of all that has gone before.

Think about it for a moment. It is not you and I who give our lives 'meaning', but rather the assessment of God: he alone is the Meaning-Maker. When life feels meaningless in patches, it is because we have not yet grasped the significance of judgment day and the revolutionary effect on our personal worldview of knowing the Judge. And if our life currently seems meaningful, but in reality we still do not know Christ personally, then it is an illusion: the 'meaning' we locate in our family, career, sport or other substitute meaning-makers is misleading and fabricated. It is not ultimate meaning, for that can derive only from God and his judgment of our lives. All meaning, in short, is defined externally to ourselves, and is not generated from within. When we make this discovery, and begin to live in the light of judgment day, it is incredibly significant.

Such then is the alternative possibility to today's popular perception that God is simply 'what we make him to be'. Often, you hear people say things like 'all religions are basically on about the same thing'. But this is like saying that all offices are basically the same: they all have a desk and a telephone, so it doesn't matter which one I go to on

Monday morning! Of course it matters. And it matters what we believe about God. Not all views of God are equally valid.

Most of all, it matters that I treat God as real. Imagine a man who goes for a job interview and believes he has won the position. Despite hearing no word, the next morning he puts on his business suit and turns up on the doorstep ready to clock on. But it is a fantasy. He has not got the job, and faces only embarrassment and disappointment. Likewise, it matters in everyday life that we act upon what is true, and not on our own fantasies. And in regard to God, the fact of judgment day makes it essential to act towards God on the basis that he is true and living.

The reality of the Judge

There can be no judgment without a judge, and this is where we get down to the core of reality. In his speech at Athens, recall that Paul said God will judge the world "by the man he has appointed" and has given proof of this "by raising him from the dead". Who is this Man who rose from the dead, who will judge everyone, and on whom everything hinges?

In the Old Testament, in Daniel chapter seven, he is spoken of as "one like a son of man coming with the clouds of heaven" (Daniel 7:13). In Daniel's narrative, this figure approaches the Ancient of Days (God) and is led into his presence, where "he is given authority, glory and sovereign power; all peoples, nations and men of every language worship him" (7:14). And here's the extent of it: "his dominion is an everlasting dominion that will not pass away, and his kingdom will never be destroyed". The New Testament in turn identifies this 'son of man' to be an historical and actual person of the first century, known as Jesus Christ. In Matthew's Gospel, Jesus repeatedly applies the 'son of man' title to himself: as lord of the sabbath (12:8), as the one who will be three days and nights in the heart of the earth (referring to the period between his death and resurrection–12:40), as the one who rules the kingdom of God and commands an army of angels (13:41), the one who will return at the second coming with the Father's glory (16:27), and the one who sits on the throne of heaven (19:28). And he will come at an hour when he is not expected (24:44).

This is Jesus Christ, the Jewish carpenter from Bethlehem who actually walked and talked on earth, and lived the life of a flesh-and-blood individual. That he is a genuine figure of history, not a figment of the imagination, is established beyond doubt. We know this because the historical description of his life and person in the New Testament is corroborated by independent sources–outside the Bible–at a number of important points. That Jesus was a genuine figure of history, that he was known as the 'Christ' and that he was executed in Judaea in the time of Pontius Pilate, are facts all attested by historians Tacitus (a Roman) and Josephus (a Jew). These historians of the period had no particular sympathy with Christianity and they therefore had no particular sympathy for the Christian message. They had no motive, in other words, to invent any stories about the man Jesus. Yet they concur with the Gospels at each point above, leaving us with no reason to doubt that Jesus was a genuine person whose life and death actually happened.

In view of this, all of a sudden the stakes are much higher for you and me, as we make up our mind about the

Christian faith. Think about it for a moment. Many people today see Christianity as like doing philosophy–just a theory, an 'airy-fairy' myth from ancient times, best left to mystics and philosophers. In fact, it is more like going into surgery: it is a practical life or death issue that concerns the real figure of Jesus Christ who lived and died, just as the Bible says he did. And as this sinks in, we begin to realise the enormity of the decision we are required to make about eternity: our response to Jesus will ultimately determine God's response to us. And our response to Jesus is not one that is made to some theory or code, but to an actual person who ate, slept and worked in real space-time on planet earth...

...Then rose bodily from the dead. Jesus did more than just live and die. He lived again. His resurrection is a crucial event we must all confront. Paul says that God has given proof of the reality of judgment day–and the authenticity of Jesus Christ–by "raising him from the dead" (Acts 17). The resurrection is not a hoax or a mystical experience; it is an historical event which we must either disprove or accept.

And disproving it is very difficult indeed: the evidence for the resurrection is simply too compelling. All four Gospels agree that Jesus rose bodily from the dead: Matthew 28:1-10, Mark 16:1-18, Luke 24:1-12, John 20:1-29. Numerous separate post-resurrection appearances are reported in the New Testament, to five hundred people at one time (1 Corinthians 15:6), to James (1 Corinthians 15:7), to the disciples (Luke 24:36), to Paul (Acts 9:5), on the road to Emmaus (Luke 24:13-32), and at Galilee on the beach (John 21:4). Many of these appearances were to hard-headed sceptics who, like Thomas, needed to be convinced of the resurrection. Importantly, the appearances were spread out over time and seen by different groups of eye witnesses, minimizing any likelihood of historical conspiracy.

Furthermore, observers have noted that the remarkable personal certainty of the apostles, exhibited for the rest of their lives as they devoted themselves to preaching the resurrection to all who would listen, was founded upon their factual experiences. Jesus showed himself alive to them "by many convincing proofs" (Acts 1:3). The word used here in the original Greek (*tekmerion*) has the meaning of demonstrable proof, and is an expression indicating the strongest type of legal evidence. Indeed, the resurrection of Jesus Christ is the foundation of apostolic Christianity: "God has raised this Jesus to life, and we are all witnesses of the fact", says Peter in Acts 2:32. Paul too was one of the eye-witnesses (Acts 9:5) and we have already seen that the content of his message in Athens was Jesus and the resurrection. For Paul, this was the heart of reality, and any other view of the world was seriously misguided.

The resurrection demonstrates the centrality, majesty and authority of Jesus, that he is the key to reality. Jesus is alive today, sitting on the throne of heaven right now as you read this.

Believing is seeing

The upshot? It matters how you and I treat him. It matters more than anything, for he is the true and living God. It means a new way of seeing that involves living in the everyday world with a view to belonging to his everlasting world.

This is when 'faith' occurs. Unlike our society, which

works according to the motto 'I've got to see it to believe it', the Bible turns this around and tells us: 'You've got to believe it to see it'. When we start to believe in the realities of eternity, judgment and Christ then we will find that we begin to see these things more and more clearly, and this in turn will alter the way we live. We will begin to live with an eye on eternity, seeking Christ when we never did before and growing less attached to the worldly loves that once so held our fascination. We will want to downsize the worldly side of life so that Christ may increase.

In this chapter, we have discussed the concrete and genuine nature of the Christian faith and have noted three things:

- the reality of eternity
- the reality of judgment day
- the reality of Jesus the Judge

A hard-headed, practical person will not ignore these realities, but take the claims of Christ seriously, and give them due examination. In the following chapters, we will explore further who Jesus is and what he came to accomplish. As we embark on this new direction, it is vital we do it on the basis of the truth about reality, as found in the Bible. Being sincere is not enough, as we saw from the example of the man who thought trains don't run on Sundays. We need instead to know the truth–the truth about Jesus–who alone can reconnect us with the one true and living God.

As the plaque on the wall in Thomas Hardy's epic *Far From the Madding Crowd* advised, "Prepare to meet thy God".

CHAPTER 5

The Monopoly of Jesus

Whim God calls us to turn from worshipping self and our home-made creed, it is not in order to worship merely another ideology but a living Being. Or as it is often put, Christianity is not a religion but a relationship, with the risen Jesus Christ.

Central to this is the call to put our 'hope' in him and no longer in the world. The Bible speaks of it as "a living hope" (1 Peter 1:3), which is set firmly and only on the risen Lord Jesus Christ, the living God, who is our Saviour (1 Timothy 4:10; Titus 2:12-13) It is the idea that we put all our eggs in his basket, placing our ultimate faith for the future in God.

If this hope is genuine, it will show itself in the way I order the priorities of my life around Christ. Putting my hope in him involves loving Jesus more than life itself; it means putting my assets, achievements and amusements in second place and putting him in first place. In short, it is an acknowledgment of the final monopoly of Jesus in all things, and will express itself in the specific arena of my own daily life.

This requires a fully accurate picture of just how pivotal Jesus is. We will be unable to put our hope in him while ever we continue to harbour a watered-down or false understanding of his place in the scheme of things.

Complex Messiah

Many people today, consciously or unconsciously, have an off-centre and diminished understanding of Jesus.

For instance, there is the popular 'good moral teacher Jesus'. A person holding this view says: "I'm ready to accept Jesus is a great ethical teacher, but I don't accept his claim to be God". A recent survey showed that two out of three people believe that "if a person is good enough, they will earn their place in heaven, regardless of religious belief". This is a very dangerous position to hold, because it fails to take account of the depth of human weakness and sinfulness, and the purity of God's holiness (and the fact that the two cannot co-exist in heaven unless something is done to deal with our sin). This view reduces the Christian gospel merely to a set of moral principles, and Jesus to just a wise moral instructor. It says, falsely, that the response we must make to God is simply to make a slightly better than average attempt to live by a good code of behaviour.

Then there is the 'therapeutic Jesus'. This is the Jesus who is better value than a psychologist, who soothes our neuroses, lifts our self-esteem and affirms that 'You're OK, I'm OK, we're all OK'. The Bible becomes a book of lullabies, and the gospel a formula for discovering inner bliss. Christianity, under this scheme, amounts to one big aspirin pill for coping with life's pressures; it becomes very human-centred rather than God-centred. The Ten Commandments become the Ten Suggestions, and God revolves around us instead of *vice versa*.

The 'Hollywood Jesus' is another one who is still lingering in the back of many people's minds. This Jesus is a mixture of the hero from the epic film *Ben Hur* starring Charlton Heston, and the sad figure of the rock opera *Jesus*

Christ Superstar. According to this version of Jesus, he was a well-meaning but tragic figure, who was idealistic but misguided. He is pictured as the 'mellow yellow' guru wearing a robe from the movies they always show on television on Good Friday. Many have trouble taking him seriously the other 364 days of the year.

Others prefer a 'give-me-what-I-want-in-life Jesus'. Whether it is prosperity, success or a new experience, this approach to Jesus is one which treats God like a supermarket item. You simply place your order and expect God to fill it on attractive terms, and when he doesn't come through, then we walk away from the Christian faith and say it "doesn't work".

Or there is the 'political Jesus'. This version appears on the political Right to champion conservative economic agendas (for example, in the Moral Majority in the US); or on the Left as a campaigner against sexism, imperialism, and global warming.

Alternatively, there is the 'ecclesiastical Jesus'. This is one of the strongest stereotypes, because many people still recall their childhood church-going or religious schooling experience, and think that Jesus lives in cathedrals and wears a monk's habit. It is easy for us to associate the name of Jesus with little more than ceremony, rites, rituals and the visible trappings of denominational institutions. Australian artist Pro Hart once did a painting that showed a bunch of people tearing a church building apart vainly looking for God; he was effectively depicting the popular misconception that God dwells somehow within the ecclesiastical structures and hierarchy of the church, and the frustration many have felt at not being able to find him there.

And there is the most subtle of all: the 'mediocre Jesus'. Probably, more than any of the others, this is the stereotype to which many succumb. This view sees Jesus as someone who can safely be ignored and who has little to say to my daily life. He is seen as trivial and beside the point. The response is to shrug our shoulders and with an apathetic tone tell ourselves, "Christianity is not worth bothering with".

This is a list of the most common counterfeits of Jesus that circulate today, and most people are influenced by them to one degree or another. What a 'complex messiah' our society seems to have invented! None of the Jesus stereotypes outlined above is, in the final analysis, worthy of our worship —or dangerous enough to arouse us from spiritual lethargy. It is no wonder that so many people are cold towards Christianity. Why would anyone give up all to follow an ecclesiastical Jesus? Or forsake everything to worship the Hollywood Jesus? These distorted versions of Jesus are simply not worth our time, let alone our wholehearted devotion. We instinctively know in our hearts that if Jesus is no more than just another politician, comedian, ceremonialist, actor, therapist, moralist or good fairy, then this cannot be the God we are meant to worship. And we certainly won't be willing to put everything else in second place.

There must be *something more* to who Jesus is, if the call to worship him and leave behind our love of near-idols is to make sense.

The kingly Jesus
That 'something more' is his kingship. A central theme in the Bible—we could even say *the* central one—is the kingdom of God. Right from the very start, in the creation account of

Genesis, there is an unmistakable emphasis on the rule of God over his creation. This is reinforced and echoed on virtually every page of Scripture. For example, 2 Samuel 7:22 says: "How great you are, O Sovereign Lord! There is no-one like you, and there is no God but you". Psalm 103:19 puts it this way: "The Lord has established his throne in heaven, and his kingdom rules over all".

In other words, the God who in the beginning created the heavens and the earth runs the whole show, the whole kit and kaboodle–everything. And the Bible, properly understood, is the record of how he has acted to display and enact his kingship down through history, even in the face of human opposition.

While God never abdicates his kingship, amazingly he is willing to selectively *delegate* it. To us. This is nothing short of astonishing. It has to be one of the most wondrous notions of all, that the Creator of the universe should see fit to bring us into his confidence and allow us to share in the running of this world, as his vice-regents. We see this occur first with Adam, who is given dominion over every living creature (Genesis 1:28). Later we see it with Moses, who is appointed leader of the people of Israel as God's spokesman (Exodus 3:10), then with the various judges who were instruments by which God brought salvation to the people from their enemies (Judges 2:16). Eventually, God delegates his authority to the kings of Israel beginning with Saul, and then most notably with David (2 Samuel 7:8) who is to be "ruler over my people Israel". At this stage of the story, God makes incredible promises to his people through David, who is told that his "throne will be established forever", and that God "will be his father and he will be my son" (2 Samuel 7:13-14).

Yet David and his successors turn out to be a deep disappointment. One after another, each of the kings of Israel fails at the point where it matters most: fidelity to God. Sin gets the better of them all–beginning with David's adultery with Bathsheba and murder of Uriah (2 Samuel 12:9), continuing with Solomon's marriage to foreign women and his apostasy with false deities (1 Kings 11:1-13), Jeroboam's golden idols for the people to worship (1 Kings 12:28), Rehoboam's introduction of worship at pagan shrines (1 Kings 14:28), and so on and so on.

By the time we reach the end of the Old Testament, the promises to David are looking very dim indeed and the 'kings' seem long gone. Only a faint expectation remains, an expectation that the true 'messiah' (meaning anointed or chosen one) may yet still arrive one day; that the ideal Davidic king figure may yet appear who will be filled with the Spirit of God and will succeed where the previous kings failed. A king to inherit the promises to David.

Nobody's puppet

Whoever this king turns out to be, one thing is for sure: the Bible says he will rule over everyone and everything, without rival. Psalm 2 is an important one to read at this point, because it makes a connection that pulls everything together. Psalm 2 is commonly known as a 'messianic' or 'enthronement' psalm and was probably used at the coronation of Israelite kings. It speaks clearly of God's chosen king. And the interesting thing is the way in which opposition to this king is equated with opposition to God himself (verses 1-2):

Why do the nations conspire and the peoples plot in vain?
The kings of the earth take their stand and the rulers
gather together against the Lord and his Anointed One.

See the correspondence? To reject God's "anointed one" (or chosen king) is the same as rejecting God himself. This reaction against God, says the psalmist, is worldwide and deliberate. In ancient times, it took the form of military attack on Israel by foreign nations or law-breaking by the king's own subjects.

In our world today, opposition to God and his chosen king takes the form of apathy or antagonism toward Jesus. And it shows itself in worldliness such as materialism, immorality, agnosticism and apathy. It amounts to essentially the same thing: a direct challenge to the authority of God himself.

The Lord's reaction is quite remarkable: he chortles! The psalm puts it this way: "The One enthroned in heaven laughs; the Lord scoffs at them". It is simply ludicrous that mere humans should presume to challenge God and his king, because the authority of God is fixed and non-negotiable. The psalmist wants his readers to appreciate how foolish it is to ignore, marginalize or otherwise resist God and his king. All our attempts at independence, our tendency to mutiny, our inbuilt disloyalty toward God (which is what the Bible means by 'sin'), no matter how cleverly disguised, are in the final analysis pathetic and futile. In God's eyes, that makes us clowns.

This brings us to the second half of Psalm 2 and its description of God's chosen ruler. Two things should strike us about this ruler. The *first* is the way his power and authority are simply given, already established: the decision to appoint him in charge of all God's empire has already been made. It is final and no correspondence will be entered into: "I have installed my King on Zion, my holy hill". This king, this anointed one, will rule with absolute authority and will crush his enemies. He is nobody's puppet, in other words. And the *second* striking feature is the intimacy between God and his king, which is spoken of using the same words that were applied to David: "He said to me, 'You are my Son; today I have become your Father'." There is a special and unique relationship between God and his messiah, like a father-son relationship. Accordingly, the son inherits the father's possession: the whole earth. And the son-king shares the good natured character of God, using his authority for the good of others and not for despotic ends.

Both sides of this king are important to our view of him: his *power* to crush those who oppose him, combined with his *love* for those who are his loyal subjects.

Planet Jesus

This king, of course, is Jesus Christ. We know this because the New Testament quotes Psalm 2 repeatedly and says that Jesus is the long-awaited ruler who finally and completely fulfills the Davidic promises. In fact, the psalm is referred to no less than six times in the New Testament:

- verses 1-2 are quoted in Acts 4:25-26, about the peoples' opposition to Jesus
- verse 7 is used in Acts 13:33, Hebrews 1:5 and Hebrews 5:5, about the Father-Son relationship
- verse 9 is quoted in Revelation 2:27 and 19:15, about how Jesus rules with an iron sceptre

There is no room for doubt: the New Testament sees Jesus as the fulfillment of Psalm 2, as the faithful ruler and divinely ordained monarch that the whole Old Testament was waiting expectantly for.

C. S. Lewis once said of Jesus that you can spit on him

as a madman, or you can fall down and worship him as Lord—but you can't call him a mere fine teacher; that option is not open to us. Jesus Christ is much, much more than simply a guru, a moral advisor, or a psychological friend. He is the Messiah King, the absolute ruler whom God has appointed in charge of all things, including you and me. He is most assuredly nobody's puppet.

Once I understand this message about the kingly Jesus, there is only one sensible response: I must then stand under it by standing under him. This means recognizing the monopoly right of Jesus to reign over me, and no longer resisting him in my daily life.

The story is told of a Greek shipping magnate who wished to show his loyalty to the King. So he asked the King's secretary, "Would His Majesty like me to give him one of my ships as a gift?". The secretary replied, "No. The King would like you to give *yourself* as the gift—then he will have all your ships as well."

This, ultimately, is what stops so many from becoming Christians. It is the real reason we resist God. Whatever else we may tell ourselves about our religious motives, this is the real one—we do not want Jesus to be our King. We do not want to give him our whole selves.

Yet there is no escaping it. In Jesus, God is making a monopoly claim on our lives to follow him. But still some might ask if this is really necessary in order to receive eternal life. Or can we gain entry to God's heavenly kingdom as our own reward? The next chapter takes up this important question.

CHAPTER 6

The Necessity of Jesus

You may have heard the story about the father who was telling his young son one day about Jesus. Struggling to find the right words that would make it crystal clear just how special Jesus is, the father suddenly thought he had a bright idea, and remarked to the boy: "Jesus is so special, it's like he is…the 'Jimi Hendrix' of life itself".

"Who is Jimi Hendrix?" asked his son. "Jimi Hendrix? Why, he's the Michael Jordan of the electric guitar!" replied the dad.

Generation gap notwithstanding, this father was trying, in his own unique style, to get across one of the core claims of the Christian faith: that Jesus is unique. In fact, in John 14:6 Jesus lays it on the line, claiming that he and nobody else can connect us with God, saying, "I am the Way, the Truth and the Life. Nobody comes to the Father except through me."

Think about this for a moment. We sometimes hear it said that while there are many religions, they all lead to the same God. Yet a moment's consideration ought to show that this cannot be true, since the various religions mutually contradict each other. That's right—the world's major faiths each make conflicting claims that are simply at odds. And Jesus, in the words above, is making the claim that he alone is the unique way to God, an exclusive claim that rules out all alternatives and effectively pits Christianity against all competing beliefs.

What makes him so necessary, so indispensable? There are two aspects to his uniqueness. The first is the *person* of Christ: he occupies a unique position in the scheme of things by virtue of who he is. There is nobody else to equal him in office and status; he is one of a kind. And the second aspect is the *work* of Christ, for when it comes to eternity we cannot save ourselves, and this makes faith in Christ totally essential. We now consider each of these aspects in turn.

The Jesus verdict

When I first saw the rock opera *Jesus Christ Superstar*, I felt that it was a very mixed bag indeed. Some of the music is very good, but the lyrics and storyline fail in a major way to do justice to the biography of Jesus Christ. The resurrection, in particular, is ignored, and the overall picture gives a very distorted version of Christ in comparison with the authentic one that we have in the New Testament. Yet when I saw it performed live on stage, despite all its faults, there was one particular scene that struck me and caused me to go home, open my Bible, and discover more of who Jesus really is. That scene was the trial of Jesus before Pontius Pilate.

Little is known of Governor Pilate's career before the year AD 26, when the Roman Emperor of the day appointed him procurator of Judaea. He came from an upper-middle-class background, and his basic religious outlook would have been formed by Roman beliefs in various deities. As the Governor stationed in Jerusalem, he had virtually total control over the affairs of the province, was commander of the occupying army, and was the highest bench of legal appeal in the area. He held the power of life and death over the citizens. He also controlled the religious life of Jerusalem, administering the Jewish Temple, its finances, and the appointment of its high priests. By any earthly measure, he was 'the man'. He had power. He had control. He decided what counted and what did not.

Or did he? The Biblical accounts in Matthew, Mark, Luke and John show another view of Pilate, as they describe the remarkable scene when Jesus was brought before him for trial. The religious leaders of the day were corrupt. They were attempting to condemn Jesus on a trumped-up charge of treason against Rome, but lacking the authority to put a man to death they had him brought before the Governor. As Pilate proceeds to question Jesus, he becomes more and more puzzled. In an attempt to test if Jesus is a political subversive, he asks him, "Are you the king of the Jews?" (Luke 23:3), but uncovers nothing offensive in Jesus and turns to the crowd saying: "I find no basis for a charge against this man".

The crowd then turns nasty, and replies in unison, "Crucify him! Crucify him!" Pilate replies, "Shall I crucify your king?". But the chief priests simply reply "We have no king but Caesar" (John 19:15). It is at this point that we see what a weak man Pilate really is. Despite his high position, he gives in to expediency at the expense of principle, and shows he is more concerned with appeasing the crowd than with justice. Trying to wash his hands of the whole affair, Pilate hands Jesus over to be crucified.

We are meant to see, however, as readers of the whole story, that it is not really Pilate who is in charge, but God. At any time he chose, Jesus could easily have called an army of angels to his side to protect him. It was Pilate who was really a pawn in the game, not Jesus. And it was Jesus who was the real king holding court, not Pilate. Yet Pilate remains responsible for his own misjudgment of Christ, making the great error of dismissing him as a nobody—without realising who he was actually dealing with.

You and I must take care not to make the same mistake. We must make the correct judgment about who Jesus is.

The Christ of Christianity

At first, it is easy to be confused and undecided about Jesus. Like Pilate, many people find that Jesus represents something of a puzzle, or a paradox. After all, most of us would agree that Jesus was a good man, probably the best that ever lived. As far as we know, he would never hurt a fly. In fact, even amongst non-church-goers today, the common view is that Jesus was at the very least a 'good teacher', a moral example for all who came after him. And this is the root of the puzzle. If Jesus was so noble, why then did the rulers of his day—and the crowd that supported them in the episode before Pilate—have Jesus put to death? What was it that got them so angry? How could such a fine man have made so many people so furious?

There was clearly something more to Jesus than just a good teacher and a fine human being. And the vital clue is found in Pilate's question of John 18:38: "What is truth?". Imagine the scene: it was a public Roman trial, presided over by the all-powerful Governor, watched by a hothouse crowd that would have included everybody who was anybody, with tough soldiers patrolling the perimeter, and the life of a man hanging in the balance. The man on trial was by now probably the most renowned figure in all Judaea. And in the middle of it all, Pontius Pilate looks at the prisoner—the prisoner, of all people!—and asks, "What is truth?".

What was it about this prisoner that prompted the mighty Pontius Pilate to ask the greatest of all questions to the least of all citizens, a mere captive? Was it the way this captive spoke, especially the things he spoke about himself? Speaking to Pilate, Jesus says: "My kingdom is not of this world. If it were, my servants would fight to prevent my arrest by the Jews. But now my kingdom is from another place" (John 18:36). When Pilate remarks "You are a king then!", Jesus replies: "You are right in saying I am a king. In fact, for this reason I was born, and for this I came into the world, to testify to the truth. Everyone on the side of truth listens to me". It is then Pilate asks, "What is truth?".

Pilate has put his finger on the nub of the matter. Here is the sticking point, the stumbling block that made the people of Jesus' day so infuriated with him. He claimed to embody the Truth. Not just to teach it, but to *be* it. He claimed to be the only Son of God. It was his claim about himself that got them mad, his claim to be none other than God. That was the one thing they would not tolerate. It was too outrageous. They hated him because he claimed to be God's Messiah.

And it is no different today: we are quite happy with Jesus up until that point, but then we part company with him. Because if Jesus is God, then that means I can no longer be captain of my own ship. All of a sudden, I have to give myself to him. Jesus claims to be the Son of God, and it is this claim that you and I must make a decision about. It is an exclusive claim, one that is intolerant of alternative views, and one that rules out a casual approach to religion.

Let me illustrate the point. Many today approach religion like they approach health and dieting. One book says it's good to have a cup of coffee a day because it fights cancer, while another book says to avoid coffee as it is bad for the stomach. One book claims regular exercise is good, but another advises never to get too strenuous. One piece of scientific advice says a glass of wine a day helps reduce cholesterol, while another says wine rots your liver. It's all so confusing—we end up throwing our hands in the air and giving up. (As the TV show *Mad About You* once advised, you might as well decide what suits you then find a book that agrees with your approach!)

Many people approach religion in the same fashion: simply decide what you want to believe about life, then find a philosophy that agrees with yours! This would be fine if the truth about God were simply a matter of opinion, but the opposite is the case. Christianity makes truth claims about who Jesus is. This is the message of the New Testament. The biographies of Jesus in Matthew, Mark Luke and John are written with the aim of establishing his uniqueness, his particularity, the fact that Jesus is like nobody else. In our pluralistic society, with its myth of relativism, it is astonishing to read the Gospels and be struck by just how distinctive Jesus is:

* *Unique in fulfilling the Old Testament.* Numerous prophecies about the Messiah figure come true in the person and work of Jesus Christ, especially the great promises to Abraham (Genesis 12:1-3) and to David (2 Samuel 7). Notably, the 'suffering servant' figure of Isaiah 53 is clearly fulfilled in Jesus, as is the 'son of man' figure of Daniel 7:13. As well, many incidental yet important expectations of the Old Testament writers are met in Jesus (see Matthew 2:17, 23; Mark 14:49; Luke 18:31; John 19:24), and several times he himself claims this (e.g. Luke 4:21).

* *Unique in superceding the Old Testament.* While there is continuity between the New Testament and the Old, there is also discontinuity because Christ is greater and permanent, unlike what came before. Hebrews 12:24 says that "Jesus is the mediator of a new covenant", making him uniquely the one we should follow. He is not simply just another great religious figure, like Abraham or Moses (or Buddha or Mohammed, for that matter); he is *the one* who surpasses all these.

* *Unique in his birth.* Mary became pregnant by the Holy Spirit of God, according to Matthew 1:18, and the Bible writers treat this matter-of-factly; they see it simply as the result of divine intervention. They regard the virgin birth to be a literal truth, because such a miracle is not difficult for the same God who created the whole universe out of nothing to begin with. It is part of the truth that makes Jesus unique.

* *Unique in his authority with miracles.* The Gospels contain numerous separate eye-witness reports of Jesus' miracles, including over 20 healings–such as the man with leprosy (Matthew 8:2-4), a paralyzed man (Mark 2:3-12), two blind men (Matthew 9:27-31), a crippled woman (Luke 13:11-13), ten men with leprosy (Luke 17:11-19) and an official's son (John 4:46-54), as well as a number of episodes where he controls the forces of nature (e.g. calming a storm in Luke 8:22-25, feeding 5000 people with a few loaves and fishes in John 6:5-13, and turning water into wine in John 2:1-11). Most remarkably, Jesus raises at least three dead people: Jairus' daughter (Matthew 9:18-19), the widow's son (Luke 7:11-15), and Lazarus (John 11:1-44).

* *Unique in his authority with words.* What struck those who heard Jesus, and distinguished his teaching from that of anybody else, was the commanding and masterful way that he spoke about life and the things of God. In Matthew we read that "the crowds were amazed at his teaching, because he taught as one who had authority" (7:29) and the same is noted by Mark (1:22) and Luke (4:32). He spoke then (and still speaks today in the words of Scripture) with authority as God. This is most starkly seen, much to the indignation of those who heard it, in his claims to have the authority to forgive human sin, a prerogative belonging to him as God. After healing the paralytic, for example, Jesus says "Son, your sins are forgiven". Hearing him say this, the local religious leaders are taken aback, asking "Why does this fellow talk like that? He's blaspheming! Who can forgive sins but God alone?" (Mark 2:7). Exactly. They had hit the nail on the head.

* *Unique in his resurrection.* All four Gospels agree that Jesus rose bodily from the grave on Sunday, after being genuinely dead on the Friday. He foretold this event before it happened (Matthew 26:61). The resurrection in turn became the cornerstone of the apostles' preaching of the Christian gospel: it forms the climax of Peter's message in Acts 2:32, and of his fellow apostles (Acts 5:30); Stephen sees the risen Jesus in Acts 7:56, providing the culmination and confirmation of his speech; while Paul meets Jesus alive on the Damascus road and goes on to champion the resurrection wherever he goes (Acts 17:31).

So we come back to Pilate's question: what is truth? The

answer is Jesus Christ. And like Pilate, we too must decide who we say Jesus is. To the ancient world, as to our world today, the truth claim of Jesus is as stark as it is unique. It is something that we must either accept or reject, for there is no middle ground. There is no-one else in his league. Jesus is one of a kind. And the upshot is that if I reject Jesus, nothing else can take his place: no other path to God, no other religion, no other way of life.

It's that sharp. Christianity takes no prisoners. It bluntly claims that reality for you and me consists of *specific fact*, not personal opinion: that there is one God, one Messiah, one plan, one choice, one version of truth, one right way to live, one great act of salvation, one climax of history, one chance at eternal life, one Bible, one way to experience God—one valid worldview.

The last innocent man

And one Saviour. This is because a stunningly unique aspect of Jesus is his perfect life: he never sinned, not even in the slightest. He always obeyed God the Father; he is the only truly innocent man who ever lived (1 John 3:5). His life was holy, unblemished and continually in harmony with the will of God and the law of God.

The significance of this is that it makes Jesus *unique in his death for the sins of the world*. The Christian gospel proclaims that Jesus is the only human being qualified to take the divine judicial penalty for the sins of others. This is what John the Baptist meant when he saw Jesus and said: "Look, the Lamb of God, who takes away the sin of the world" (John 1:29). In the Old Testament, a sacrificial lamb without blemish or imperfection was at different times offered as an atonement for sins (e.g. Leviticus 14:10-13). It was a ceremony instituted by God for cleansing from defilement and forgiveness of sin. In the New Testament, it is then made clear that under the new covenant, Jesus is now the full and final atoning sacrifice for our sins (1 John 2:2). By virtue of his perfectly obedient life, Jesus is a "lamb without blemish or defect" (1 Peter 1:19). This means that Jesus alone qualifies to wipe away our sins because, unlike us, he is blameless.

It is like we are broken appliances, and only one repairman in the universe can fix us. What is broken? Answer: we are. And why are we broken? Answer: because of our sin against Almighty God. And who alone can repair it? Answer: Jesus Christ.

Forgiven trespasses

How serious is the problem of sin? Very. We all tend to grossly underestimate the scandal of our sin in the sight of God. Sin can be defined as self-centredness; it is a challenge to the position of God. At first blush, perhaps we don't feel particularly self-centred. No more than the next guy at least. But if the truth be known, and as the chapters earlier in this book have sought to demonstrate, we are in fact self-absorbed. Our daily lives are full of love of the world and of self, dominated by the secular mindset in which God and the gospel of his kingdom are not counted as the *primary reality*. Instead we allow other loyalties to take over, pursuits of ordinary living that are innocent in themselves but deadly in the way we all get distracted by them. Hence the apostle Paul defines Christian conversion as "turning from idols to serve the true and living God" (1 Thessalonians 1:9).

It counts for nothing that we are civilised and nice people.

Ask yourself this question: does a sincere and well-mannered thief who breaks into your home make you feel any better about it than an ill-mannered one? Of course not. And so too with our attempt to ransack the kingdom of God. Our offences of immorality and world-love amount to a denial of God. 'Meaning well' counts for little. Because of sin, the knots in our rope remain and only Jesus can untie them.

The list of our world-loving and God-denying behaviours is long and serious. Here are just a few, drawn from our earlier chapters:

- Instead of treasuring the word of God, we make up our own philosophy of life, fed partly by countless hours paying homage to the 'gospel according to Hollywood' through television and movies.

- Instead of valuing our spiritual fitness above all else, we live and breath sport.

- Instead of seeing work as simply a daily occupation under God, we make it a defining preoccupation from which our sense of identity is derived.

- Instead of seeking first to develop inner character, we are mesmerized by outward charm.

- Instead of hanging loose to material possessions, we measure our progress in life by accumulating them.

- Instead of keeping our family in perspective as a gift from God, we make it first priority in our lives even at the expense of knowing God.

And so on. Like a game of musical chairs, a life of chasing the world amuses us for a time—but when the music stops, what then?

When the music stops, we face the judgment of God. Like the famous 'Checkpoint Charlie' that guarded the border between West and East Berlin for many decades, there is Another Checkpoint through which those crossing from this life into the next must pass, the day of reckoning with God.

Don't leave home without him

All of this is what makes Jesus essential. Jesus is unique in being both fully God and fully Man. He is the only Son of God, shown by his recorded life and works which are unlike any other. This makes it essential to acknowledge him as Lord. And he is the only human being to be without sin, making his death on the cross essential to Christian belief and making it absolutely necessary for each of us to personally know him as Saviour.

There is a painting in a museum in Amsterdam called *The Meditation.* Painted by The Master of Spes Nostra, it depicts four people praying at the edge of an open grave. The decaying corpse is clearly visible. In the background, by contrast, are scenes of everyday life, happy blissful snapshots such as children playing, minstrels singing, and young women adorned in all their beauty. It is the contrast, almost surreal in its effect, which shocks the viewer, that of a sharp clash between everyday joys and the gloom of the funeral scene. The artist is urging us to reflect on the reality of our mortality and not be fooled by how good life may seem to be on the surface while we are still young. We are meant to meditate on the transitory nature of life.

The Bible says with certainty about the future that "man is destined to die once, and after that to face judgment" (Hebrews 9:27). We are all in the same boat, on the same sea, facing the same storm. As someone once said of the Saviour, "only those drowning can see him", and it is when we appreciate for the first time the full reality of our sin and our inability to rescue ourselves, that we then understand the necessity of Jesus.

CHAPTER 7

The Sufficiency of Jesus

The story is told that when St Paul's Cathedral in London was being built, some of those involved did not feel fully confident that the structure could support itself.

Despite being designed by England's most respected architect, Christopher Wren, when the plans were submitted to city council, the councillors ordered that an additional central pillar be added, from ground level all the way up to the high point of the main dome. This, they said, was needed to provide support lacking in the original design. Despite his absolute confidence in the sufficiency of the building structure, Wren had little choice but to oblige their request and the pillar was added.

Many years afterwards, in the late nineteenth century, renovations were being carried out on the Cathedral when a startling feature of the controversial pillar came to light for the first time: it actually never reached the top of the dome, but instead stopped short by about a centimetre. In actual fact, it supported nothing. Wren's original structure was sufficient after all, yet the councillors had doubted him—and in so doing insulted him.

This story illustrates what can go wrong with our thinking about God, and especially our understanding of the Christian doctrine of salvation. God has designed the way for men and women to be saved through Christ, and his design is complete for us. Yet we all too easily fall into the trap of wanting to add our own 'extras' to God's plan, like bits of additional insurance. When we do this, it amounts to a slap in the face to God because we are implying that the work of Jesus alone is not enough to secure our salvation.

Although Jesus has (in the famous words of the Anglican Prayer Book) made a "full, perfect and sufficient sacrifice for the sins of the whole world", people today often find it difficult to fully entrust themselves to him. They are tempted to add their own 'safety devices'—things like church-going, respectability, morality, good works, charity, baptism, confirmation, holy communion, a tolerant outlook, and most of all a pinch of effort to be basically a fair or nice person. Deep down, many struggle to believe that God can forgive us on a basis entirely removed from any of these things, but in doing so they are implicitly doubting God and effectively insulting him.

To guard against this error, the sixteenth century Reformers like Martin Luther used the phrase *sola Christo*: 'Christ alone' for salvation. If we are trusting in anything instead of, or in addition to, the death of Jesus on the cross for forgiveness, we nullify his death and come up empty. It is therefore important, if we are to be a Christ-lover, that we rid our thoughts of alternative theories of God's acceptance of us, embracing instead the cross of Jesus Christ alone.

Won by One

The principle of the sole sufficiency of Jesus Christ for our salvation was famously explained in 1545 by Martin Luther in an autobiographical fragment included in the preface to a collection of his complete works:

*Although I lived a blameless life as a monk, I felt that I
was a sinner with an uneasy conscience before God. I also
could not believe that I had pleased him with my works.
Far from loving that righteous God who punished sinners,
I actually hated him… At last, as I meditated day and
night on the relation of the words (in Romans 1:17,
3:22) "the righteousness of God is revealed in it, as it is
written, the righteous person shall live by faith", I began
to understand the 'righteousness of God' as that by which
the righteous person lives by the gift of God (faith)…
This immediately made me feel as though I had been born
again, and as though I had entered through open gates
into paradise itself.*

You can sense the excitement in Luther's words as he
discovers for himself the 'free gift' of salvation that the
Bible teaches. Suddenly a great weight is lifted. He no
longer hates the idea of God's perfect holiness, but now
regards 'the righteousness of God' as a most wonderful
thing: "I began to love and extol it as the sweetest of
phrases" writes Luther. He sees for the first time how salvation is entirely God's work, not ours.

It is this realisation that has such a revolutionary impact
on our standing before God. Before the penny dropped for
him, Luther thought that sinners got right with God as an
act of human achievement, by their own moral effort. Yet
he was unsettled about this, because—even living the life of
a good monk—he knew that his sins remained great. He
doubted that God would accept him.

After his discovery from the Bible of the principle of
'justification by faith', Luther realised that being right with
God is not something we give God, but is something God
gives us. Previously, he saw the righteousness of God only

as a judging righteousness. Now, he saw its other side: as a saving righteousness.

Here's a test of whether you and I, like Luther, have personally grasped the doctrine known as 'justification by grace through faith in Jesus Christ alone': at this moment, are you certain of your salvation? Do you have that sense of ironclad assurance that you are right with God, or is it more that you 'hope that God will accept you into heaven'? If we are relying in any way on ourselves to find acceptance in God's sight, then we will lack that sense of assurance. If instead we are relying on the finished work of Jesus, then we can rest assured our eternity is secure. When we finally grasp the one true way of salvation in Christ, then (and only then) we find assurance of it.

Alongside this, furthermore, there should be a corresponding deep aversion to our own sinfulness. There is an inverse correlation between our personal appreciation of sin and our grasp of God's grace: the more we apprehend our own tendency toward error and wrongdoing, the more we become convinced of our inability to save ourselves, and in turn, the more we will cast ourselves fully onto the cross of Jesus Christ for salvation. So we must honestly ask ourselves this question: have I perceived the depth of my own worldliness? Do I see the full extent of my sin: ignoring God, defying his commands, seeking to be independent of him, worshipping created things in place of the Creator, being self-absorbed and doubting his word, the Bible?

Once we truly see the work of Jesus Christ in saving us, it is a fact of incredible awe and wonder. Like the New Testament writer of Galatians, we will be overwhelmed by "the Son of God, who loved me and gave himself for me" (2:20). Christianity all of a sudden will mean more to us than mere religion; it will be much more than just dry theory; it will ring with the reality of God's saving love. An old hymn captures this well:

> *And can it be, that I should gain*
> *An interest in the Saviour's blood?*
> *Died he for me, who caused him pain,*
> *For me, who him to death pursued?*
> *Amazing love! How can it be*
> *That thou, my God, should die for me?*

This will change forever the 'aspirations' we talked about in earlier chapters. It is here that we find the power to give up our modern day 'idols'. As our hearts are moved by the discovery that Jesus alone, through his death and resurrection, has secured for us everlasting life, then our existing attachments begin to fade. Another famous hymn captures this shift: "Turn your eyes upon Jesus, look full in his wonderful face, and the things of earth will grow strangely dim, in the light of his glory and grace". All the vain things of daily life that previously charmed us most, we will become increasingly willing to sacrifice for the sake of knowing him better. No longer will it seem worthwhile to pursue our old obsessions, because now the true and living God has captured our imagination. The saving work of Jesus Christ, in other words, is the one factor strong enough to make us willingly resign our past preoccupation with self-centred priorities, as we turn our eyes more and more to him.

God does not leave us to do this on our own. He pours out his Holy Spirit on the new believer, enabling us to live for him (Romans 8:1-14, 26). By God's Spirit, we not only receive new life, but the power to live a new lifestyle (Galatians 5:16-25). God sends his Spirit to dwell within us, and to progressively produce in us the characteristics that are pleasing to God. So we do not have to turn from our old way of life by our own strength; rather, God comes to our aid, transforming us by the renewal of our minds (Romans 12:1-2).

Clear Christianity

The teaching of the sufficiency of Christ for salvation is such a rich concept that it calls for some technical words to capture it better. Although some of these may be unfamiliar, they can help make us a lot clearer on the adequacy and finality of Jesus' work in saving us.

The death and resurrection of Jesus accomplishes the following.

- *justification*: the New Testament makes it clear that because of the death and resurrection of Christ, the believer is made 'right with God' (Romans 3:24-26, 1 Peter 3:18). Justification is an image drawn from a law court, and implies that the status of the believer has been reversed—from being under God's legal judgment for breaking his law, to being declared acquitted by God. Justification is therefore the opposite of condemnation. God no longer counts our sins against us, instead accounting us righteous on the basis of Christ's life and death (Romans 5:1, 8:1).

- *propitiation*: as sinners, we are under the anger of God and face the full force of his fury because of our wrongful treatment of him. In Christ, however, the wrath of God is averted, or 'propitiated'. Christ stands in as our substitute, and takes God's anger towards sinners upon himself on the cross, so that those who put their trust in him have nothing to fear (Romans 3:25).

- *reconciliation*: in sections of the New Testament such as 2 Corinthians 5:14-21 and Colossians 1:19-23, it is clear that on the basis of Christ's death and resurrection we can be reconciled to God. This means we are changed from his enemies into his friends. In Christ, God was reconciling us to himself and not counting our sins against us, which means removing any sense of quarrel or enmity and establishing renewed friendship.

- *redemption*: the force of this commercial metaphor is that God, through giving his only Son to die on the cross, has purchased the Christian at a high price. He has bought us back, at great expense to himself (Ephesians 1:7; 1 Corinthians 6:19-20). It carries the idea of being ransomed, where the asking price is Christ's own death, who came to be "a ransom for many" (Mark 10:45). In the time of Jesus, it was connected with the commonplace act of redeeming the life of someone by paying a sum of money, especially purchasing freedom for a slave.

  You and I are pictured in the Bible as 'slaves to sin' (John 8:34) who regain our freedom through Christ.

All these descriptions in their different ways show Christ as being like a bridge between sinners and a holy God. Let me illustrate. Between Thailand and Laos, there is a new and amazing bridge. Built in the early 1990s, it is a very long bridge, a remarkable feat of engineering that stretches for more than one kilometre, and so spans a distance that for a long time acted as a barrier to all who wished to cross. It's almost a 'miracle' of construction that for many years was thought impossible. More than that, it is a bridge that connects two different countries, bringing together foreigners and making them friends. In fact, it is called exactly that: the 'Friendship Bridge', which again is a handy image of the bridge that Christ alone provides between us and God, that everlasting bridge that allows us to dwell in God's country.

All in all, the cross is the place where Jesus heals the rift between God and sinners like us. The alienation from God that we caused has been dealt with—once and for all—by the infinite worth of Jesus' payment for the sins of the world.

Just Jesus

There is one more word we ought to know in understanding the sufficiency of Christ for salvation, and that is *satisfaction*. This word captures the idea that Jesus has fully satisfied the requirements of God for the salvation of wayward world-lovers like you and me. There is nothing more that remains to be done, nothing else that can be added, no other offering that needs to be made.

How do we know this is the case? Because of the resurrection of Jesus. By raising him from the dead, God was putting his stamp of approval on his Son and declaring that Christ's work was finished and complete. The resurrection was God's way of showing that Jesus had conquered death. It is his acceptance of the death of Christ as being sufficient and total in its effect of saving the believer. It was a grand public display of God's 100% approval of Jesus who died for us.

The resurrection is therefore vitally important in showing the sufficiency of Jesus for our future security. In raising Jesus, and in thus affirming him as the king who has triumphed over all his enemies (sin, death, Satan and those who do not believe), God is saying to the world that Christ has all authority in heaven and on earth to forgive sins. We can therefore be totally confident that trusting in the death and resurrection of Jesus Christ alone will guarantee everlasting life. Jesus is, in a word, sufficient.

CHAPTER 8

The Attraction of Jesus

Douglas Copeland, the man who coined the term 'Generation X' and first drew our attention to the rise of 'irony' in modern thinking, has openly admitted his struggle to make sense out of a world where all that happens, whether good or bad, is summed up as simply 'ironic'. In his third book, *Life After God* (1994), he writes about this through the eyes of one character, who says, "I'm trying to escape from ironic hell. I'm trying to turn cynicism into faith; randomness into clarity; worry into devotion".

Copeland seems to be saying it is not easy living in our society today, because it has only one explanation for everything that happens to us: irony. He's right. When there is no longer a place for God in our hearts, irony is all that is left to make sense of it all, and life starts to feel like a cheap takeaway meal that leaves you hungry again in half an hour. So there is absolutely no doubt in my mind that one of the main consequences of our society's rejection of God is a deep unspoken dissatisfaction and spiritual thirst.

In contrast, Christianity holds out the promise of lasting purpose and meaning. Peace. Joy. Contentment. Eternal security. These are priceless, and yet so many people today strive in vain without ever finding them. Without them, we cannot know true satisfaction and will go on trying to quench our thirst with worldly things. As described in chapter 2, we will remain subject to futility. Like a ship-wrecked man who has only saltwater to drink, our quasi-idolatry delivers only thirst and more thirst. In the movie *The American President*, starring Michael Douglas as the President, one of the presidential advisors makes a speech highlighting the search for purpose in our world today: "The people want leadership. They're so thirsty for it they'll crawl through the desert toward a mirage and when they discover there's no water, they'll drink the sand." He's right. We yearn for water to drink that will quench our spiritual thirst, but so much of the time we come up with only a mirage, not the real thing.

This is what makes Jesus such an attractive alternative. It might sound like a cliché, but following Jesus offers this big attraction: he satisfies the soul in a way that the world never can.

Living water

In the New Testament, there is an episode where Jesus arrives at a town called Sychar, in an area known as Samaria, some distance from Jerusalem (see John chapter 4). He has a conversation there with a woman he meets by a well. The people of Samaria were hated by the Jews, who refused to have anything to do with them. God, however, had not given up on the Samaritans, for he loves all of us and wants people of all nations to turn to him to be saved.

When the Samaritan woman came to draw water, Jesus said to her: "Will you give me a drink?".

She replied, "You are a Jew and I am a Samaritan woman. How can you ask me for a drink?" Not only did Jews not associate with Samaritans, but men often did not associate with women, and this made Jesus' question a double puzzle to her.

Jesus answered her: "If you knew the gift of God and who it is that asks you for a drink, you would have asked him and he would have given you living water". She thinks Jesus is talking about water in the everyday sense, and so queries his words: "Sir, you have nothing to draw with and the well is deep. Where can you get this living water?"

Now Jesus makes a startling claim: "Everyone who drinks this water will be thirsty again, but whoever drinks the water I give him will never thirst. Indeed the water I give him will become in him a spring of water welling up to eternal life."

Jesus is not talking about everyday water–he is now talking about 'everlasting water'. What does it mean?

Only one person is qualified to offer everlasting water, the kind that gives us eternal life, and that person is God. We know this from the Old Testament, where the image of water is used of the salvation and life that God gives to those who know him. For instance, Isaiah says "with joy you shall draw water from the well of salvation" (12:3; see also Zechariah 14:8). So when Jesus uses the term it has this Old Testament background. Yet there's more to it now, because Jesus is openly claiming that *he* is the one who gives this 'living water' of salvation.

The Samaritan woman, after being told some details about her personal life that no stranger could have known except by divine knowledge, finally starts to come around. She stops worrying about natural water and begins reflecting upon the supernatural water Jesus is speaking about. "I know the Messiah is coming", she says, to which Jesus replies: "I who speak to you am he".

Like this woman, we too must drink of the living water that meets the need of our souls, by going to Christ for it. Jesus can satisfy our greatest need—for eternal life and salvation from sin—because he is none other than God. When Christ gives us his living water, not only does it meet our constitutional need—to be forgiven and sustained in everlasting life—but it also meets our existential need, to find fulfillment and direction day by day. Isaiah 58:11 puts it this way:

> *The Lord will guide you always;*
> *he will satisfy your needs in a sun-scorched land*
> *and will strengthen your frame.*
> *You will be like a well-watered garden,*
> *like a spring whose waters never fail.*

Not knowing Christ is to be thirsty and dissatisfied, lost and unsaved. Knowing Christ is life and peace, because we know we are secure in God. We can live simply yet abundantly, without the need for desperate quests such as materialism or careerism to make us feel better or to convey an artificial purpose for living. As Jesus said, "I have come that you might have life, and have it abundantly" (John 10:10).

There is nothing so satisfying as being in tune with our Creator again, having his Holy Spirit within us, growing to be like Christ, belonging to the people of God at our church, feeding on his word the Bible, and having the assurance of eternal salvation with him.

Knowing God's Joy

All of this, say the Scriptures, is the formula for real happiness in life. As we noted in an earlier chapter, the *Westminster Confession* sums up the meaning of life with the idea of

"enjoying" God "forever". The Bible rings with the theme
of true joy, and says that there is only one Person who can
really give it to us: God.

Psalm 33 is a good example. It begins with the startling
idea that joy is a command:

> *Sing joyfully to the Lord, you righteous;*
> *it is fitting for the upright to praise him.*

It's a funny idea–that joy might be a command, not an
option, and much less a chance event that depends on
some notion of fate. Deep joy is "fitting" for us when we
come to know God, just like it is for a bride on her wedding
day, or for a father holding his newborn child for the first
time. There is an underlying quality of fulfillment that
derives from knowing God and being in right relationship
with our Creator, and it should give rise to a no-holds-
barred gladness with life that simply wells up inside us.

What is the foundation for this God-given joy? The
Psalm gives four axioms on which true and lasting joy is
founded, like the four points of a compass.

First, permanent joy is grounded upon *the word of God*
(verses 4-9). His word brought forth creation. By simply
speaking, God made 'the heavens'. The stars were made by
the breath of his mouth, and by his powerful word God
gathers the waters of the sea 'into jars':

> *For he spoke and it came to be,*
> *he commanded and it stood firm (verse 9).*

The power of God's spoken word is seen in what Louis
Armstrong famously called this 'wonderful world', and
should cause us to fear the Lord and 'revere him' (verse 8).
The Psalm then refers to the word of God in judgment, and

especially its 'justice' and 'righteousness'. The writer of the psalm is reminding us of the fidelity and reliability of God's character, so that by putting our trust in his word we can know we are living by what is true. This should cause us to be filled with joy, because one day everything that is wrong with our world will be put right, and all who are believers in the promises of God will be vindicated.

The second foundation given for joy is *the plan of God* (verses 10-11). Human beings make plans, just like God does. This is one of the aspects of being 'created in the image of God'. But our plans are tainted by sin. Ultimately, because we all oppose God and make self-centred plans, by ourselves and apart from him, our plans will fail (verse 10): "The Lord foils the plans of the nations; he thwarts the purposes of the peoples". Ultimately failed plans do not produce joy.

Ask yourself this question: What has become of all the people alive in the year 1900? Or 1800? What came of their great plans? Today, they are gone. Their plans have come to nothing, their assets owned by others, their achievements forgotten. The same will eventually be true of all those alive in the year 2000. Human plans fade like grass at the end of summer, but God's plans will stand the test of time (verse 11):

But the plans of the Lord stand firm forever,
The purposes of his heart through all generations.

God is carrying out his scheme for salvation, and is establishing his kingdom with an unswerving focus. This in turn produces a profound joy once we know that we are part of it.

The third reason for joy is *the sovereignty of God* (12-19). The Bible pictures God like a master cosmic chess player who is sovereign over every move in the game of life, right through to its conclusion. He knows what moves each of us will make before we make them—indeed he ordains everything that happens in his world. He already sees the 'end-game', in which Christ will reign and Satan will finally be crushed. This is meant to be a great source of joy, once we become Christians, because it says that God chose us before we chose him, and he holds onto us more firmly and everlastingly than we could ever hold onto him. The psalm says that God has chosen his people to be his personal inheritance, and elsewhere in the Bible the Christ-follower is called a 'child' of God, an heir to the promises of God, and what greater joy can there be than this?

Finally, we can have great joy based on *the love of God* (18-19). Like a father caring for his children, or a shepherd for his sheep, God has what the psalm writer calls an "unfailing love" (18). This is a terrific ground for hope, defined not as a vague wish that the unlikely might occur, but as a certain expectation that what is promised to us in Christ will indeed come to fruition. God is loving and faithful: all who honour him, he will uphold, sustain and deliver.

Now we understand why the psalmist can 'command' joy. In the closing verses of Psalm 33, we have it summed up:

In him our hearts rejoice for we trust in his holy name.

See the logic? Faith in God is the central command of Scripture, and authentic faith will always generate true and lasting joy in the believer. The two go hand in hand, and so making joy a command is just as natural to the Bible writers as making faith a command. Faith—a reliance on God—will produce deep, joyous, lasting contentment in God.

The attraction of Jesus

Is this kind of joy our experience? Joy in the biblical sense is not a matter of personality, but of character. It is much more lasting than the feeling of a kid with a new bike on Christmas morning, or the smiling faces on new car advertisements. It is much deeper than mere mirth or merriment, or a jolly smile. It is not something our worldly pursuits can ever give.

Rather, Christian joy is the satisfaction of the soul in attaining its true design and arriving at its true home, in Christ. It does not mean our life will be free from trouble, nor that we will never feel melancholy. But in the midst of life's circumstances, however difficult, it means we have a sure hope. Spurgeon spoke of the Christian's "humble hope", and there is no other philosophy that features joy so prominently in its teaching as Christianity. No other could. This is the attraction of Jesus Christ, in a society that has become addicted to mere shadows of the real thing.

PART 3

Seeking First His Kingdom

CHAPTER 9

The Turning Point

While driving home recently at around 10:30 pm one night, I was listening to the late night personal advice show on radio. I heard from one deserted husband how his wife of ten years suddenly decided she wanted out of the relationship, and so simply left a yellow 'post-it' note stuck on the fridge and left without any further word of explanation. In another tragic story, a man told his wife he needed to 'go find himself' then took the Saab and left, leaving her with the Toyota, the kid and the mortgage. Another caller told how he stepped out to go down to the corner store, leaving his best mate in the house with his wife of twenty-one years; when he came back a few minutes later, they were gone, run away together.

At the risk of sounding clichéd, we live in a world where love has gone wrong, seriously wrong. It is wider than just marriages: there is a loss of community and a breakdown of trust, between parent and child, between boss and worker, between teacher and student, between neighbour and friend.

Over time, this has a grinding effect on us. We slowly lose faith in others, in the possibility of real love, in faith itself. As a well-known folk poem puts it, when a person lives with criticism for long enough, they learn to condemn;

when a person lives with betrayal, they learn not to trust; when a person lives with being ignored, they learn to feel worthless. Deep down we know that love is supposed to be our experience, for we are built for it by the God who made us. But we have been hurt too many times, and have become cynical. Our hearts have become hard and dry, like an over-boiled egg.

Some respond to these harsh experiences by closing up like a clam, bringing down the emotional shutters and retreating to an inner personal safety zone where they can play it safe. The problem with this is that without genuine love, we freeze on the inside, and life loses its warmth and sweetness. Others make the opposite mistake, of trying to buy love. They treat love as a commodity that can be exchanged, and spend their lives desperately trying to bargain for the attention and affection of others (including God) in some kind of contractual marketplace of the heart. But here too there is a fatal problem, for as soon as the love of others must be earned, it is no longer love.

Inevitably, we turn to pseudo-idols, like those we talked about in earlier chapters. When we do not know the love of God, we try loving the world instead. But it never satisfies.

The way back to God

It doesn't have to be this way. The Bible says: "This is how we know what love is: Jesus Christ laid down his life for us" (1 John 3:16). The promise of God is that if we throw in our lot with him, he will never let us down, because he is totally trustworthy and his character fully reliable. We don't need to settle for second best any more.

To illustrate the radical and stunning nature of God's love, Jesus told a story about a man who had two sons

THE TRUE AND LIVING GOD

(in Luke 15:11-24). The younger one says to his father, "Father, give me my share of the estate". So the father divides his property between his sons. Not long after that, the younger son gets together all he has, sets off for a distant country and there squanders his wealth in wild living.

This decision by the son to leave home is a metaphor for how we each treat God when we try to be agnostic, enjoying all the good things his world has to offer but not paying any serious attention to him. Of course, we probably doff our cap to him occasionally, like the son who probably sent an occasional postcard to his father from time to time. But if the truth be known, we have gone off to a distant spiritual country, worshipping the idols in our lives—entertainment, sport, work, charm, money, family—instead of our Creator.

Jesus continues his story. After the son has spent everything, there is a severe famine in that whole country, and he begins to be in need. So he goes and hires himself out, and finds himself working in the fields feeding the pigs. He is so hungry, he longs to fill his stomach with the pods the pigs are eating, but no-one gives him anything.

It is at this point, when his own resources are exhausted, that he comes to his senses and begins to entertain the idea of returning to his father. Only this time, it would be as a servant, not a son. He says to himself, "How many of my father's hired men have food to spare, and here I am starving to death! I will set out and go back to my father and say to him: 'Father, I have sinned against heaven and against you. I am no longer worthy to be called your son; make me like one of your hired men.'" And so he turns for home.

This is how it happens—becoming a Christian, that is. It is only when we understand our poverty without God that we see the need to come begging to him. Only a drowning man sees the life saver. This is the start of repentance. It requires a renunciation of our own resources, good works and self-sufficiency. And it means we break with the pursuit of worldliness. No longer do we try to be independent of God and keep him at arms length. Instead, realising our total inability to have a future without God, we arise and come to Christ. The son in the story had to learn humility and surrender his independence before he could see how good things had been back home.

What happens next in the story is amazing. It truly is a message of amazing grace.

While the son is still a long way off, his father sees him and is filled with compassion for him; he runs to his son, throws his arms around him and kisses him. The son says, "Father, I have sinned against heaven and against you. I am no longer worthy to be called your son".

But the father says to his servants, "Quick! Bring the best robe and put it on him. Put a ring on his finger and sandals on his feet. Bring the fattened calf and kill it. Let's have a feast and celebrate. For this son of mine was dead and is alive again; he was lost and is found." And they begin to celebrate.

What has always struck me is the extravagance of the father in this story, who represents God. The kind of love on view here is not what we are used to. It is covenant love, not contractual love. You don't earn it, you just marvel at it, and gratefully embrace it. In fact, you let it wash over you, and if it makes you want to punch the air with delight then go right ahead.

God specialises in extreme love, the kind that is wild and unexpected, so surprising and unconventional that it takes your breath away. His love is improbable and very costly. That is what makes it so precious, so priceless–and so life changing.

At Mount Gambier there are some 'sink holes', volcanic wells in the ground that formed naturally and are very deep. In fact, they are so deep that geologists have been unable to fathom the depth of them, to reach the bottom. They appear bottomless. And this is what God's love is like: you never reach the bottom of it. It is infinite. It is larger than we ever imagined. Indeed the New Testament says that we need the power of God's Spirit to grasp "how long and wide and high and deep is the love of Christ" (Ephesians 3:18).

Like the father in the story, God wants to call each of us sons and daughters. Why settle for less?

A change of heart

How do I respond to the promise of God in Jesus Christ, and take hold of God's love for my own life? Three steps.

First, *look inward.*

Like the prodigal son, I must look inside and acknowledge that I am a sinner because I have gone away from God and done my own thing in life. I have loved 'idols' more than I have loved him, and have all too often tried to be independent of Jesus Christ. In the words of Humphrey Bogart in the film *Barefoot Contessa,* "When I was a kid I had two choices: everyone wanted me to be a good little boy and be nice to others; I chose to be a bad little boy and be nice to myself". This describes us to a tee.

God says the penalty for our sin is death and hell (Revelation 20:10-15, Matthew 25:46), and we must be brutally honest with ourselves and with God at this point. Most of the time, our running away from God has not taken an 'active' form—like being Adolph Hitler, or murder, or being the school bully. Rather, it mostly takes a 'passive' form: gossip, greed, apathy, hypocrisy, racism, anger, deceit, lust, discord, selfish ambition, insensitivity, stubbornness, being uncooperative, manipulation, lies, pride, envy, false pretences, jealousy, factionalism, cold-heartedness, and so on and so on.

The list is endless. Our sin might be sophisticated and respectable, but it makes us guilty just the same. As outlined in Part I, our lives are riddled with idolatry as we pursue the created things rather than the Creator himself, and this is an offence in the sight of God that is punishable by death and hell.

Second, realising we are under judgment, we must *look upward.*

This means looking to Christ as our one sure hope for salvation, for "there is no other name under heaven by which we can be saved" (Acts 4:12). We need to recognize that this is why Jesus came, to die on the cross in our place to take the penalty for our sin. As Romans 5:8 puts it, "God demonstrates his own love for us in this: while we were still sinners, Christ died for us".

A few years ago I had the opportunity to preach in a Russian womens' prison. As I was waiting in the Warden's office to meet the bilingual translator for the occasion (I do not speak Russian!), in walked a woman in her forties. She looked like a regular middle-class person, dressed in street clothes and showing a high level of education.

I asked her if she worked at the gaol, and she replied, "No, in actual fact I am one of the inmates".

I said, "Do you mind if I ask what you are in for?".

"Not at all", she said, "I'm serving a sentence for murder".

I gulped and took a deep breath: "Oh really, murder?".

"Yes, that's right", she continued, "I came home one night to find my husband in bed with his lover, and in a rage I killed them both. Now I'm serving ten years."

It was what she said next that amazed me. "Before I came into the prison, I was not religious. But I began attending the prison Bible study led by the chaplain, and came to understand the gospel, and accepted Jesus Christ as my Lord and Saviour. I now know I am pardoned by God, in spite of my crime, through Jesus' death on the cross, and it is a great pleasure and a privilege to act as interpreter for your meeting today."

With that, we left the warden's office and entered a large hall full of several hundred women prisoners. It struck me then that when you speak the Christian gospel to a group of convicted criminals, you don't need to work very hard to convince them they are sinners! I will never forget the look on the faces of those inmates as they heard the message of forgiveness of sins by God's grace through faith in Jesus Christ: their eyes lit up and I believe that for many, many women that day it was the very first time they saw the truth of the gospel.

If God can forgive criminals who turn to Christ, then he can also forgive mild-mannered people when they do the same.

Third, when becoming a Christian we need to do what the prodigal son did and *look homeward*.

That is, commit ourselves to returning to God who is our heavenly Father. This is the test of whether we really want to love Christ, or whether we are kidding ourselves. When Jesus was asked to say which is the greatest of all God's commandments, he answered, "The most important one is this...Love the Lord your God with all your heart and with all your soul and with all your mind and with all your strength" (Mark 12:29-30), and the message of this book is exactly that, namely, the need for God to be 'Priority One' in our lives.

Importantly, coming back to the family fold will also mean being part of the community of God, his church. Jesus continues: "And the second is this: Love your neighbour as yourself" (Mark 12:31). The prodigal knew that he had to swallow his pride and return to his father's house. Jesus tells us to love each other as "I have loved you" (John15:12). In other words, our commitment to other Christians is tied closely to our commitment to Jesus Christ. The two principles go together. When people say today "I can be a Christian without going to church", they are therefore failing to make the vital connection between Christ and his church. As going to the bank is connected with saving, and visiting the supermarket goes with eating, so church is linked with faith in Christ. We can no more live the Christian life without belonging to church, than we can drive a car without ever stopping in at petrol stations.

Becoming a Christian means renouncing the 'idol' of individualism. In the Bible's view, a Christian without a church is like a bee without a hive, or a sailor without a ship, or a footballer without a team. In God's way of thinking, believing always implies *belonging*. Church is the Carpenter's workshop, where Jesus of Nazareth reshapes our character and smooths off the rough edges, fashioning us into his likeness as we interact with fellow believers. It is where we learn to be tolerant, to be patient, to not be self-engrossed, to show compassion—in short, it is where we learn to love (1 John 3:16). (We will come back to this in chapter 12.)

Turning to God

In summary, becoming a follower of Jesus involves:

- looking inward–to recognize I am a sinner in God's sight

- looking upward–to embrace God's Son Jesus as my saviour

- looking homeward–to return to God the Father, in a new relationship of trust and obedience

This leaves us with a choice between two futures: remaining in the grip of the world and indifferent to the claims of Jesus, or turning to Jesus as Lord and Saviour, becoming indifferent to the claims of the world. It is the second path that God urges us to take–"to escape the corruption of the world by knowing our Lord and Saviour Jesus Christ" while we still can (2 Peter 2:20).

I want to ask you the question: Where does the accent fall in your life? What is your heart set on? God challenges each of us to become committed disciples of Christ. Perhaps you are a 'nominal Christian' who now realises the reality has been missing from your commitment to Christ, a churchgoer who needs to move from mere ritual to genuine discipleship. Or perhaps you have been a non-Christian, or even an anti-Christian, but now God is speaking to your heart–and you know the time has come to start listening.

In the New Testament, God called on people to "turn from idols to serve the true and living God" in the person of Jesus Christ. And today he calls on everyone to turn from worldly goals and aspirations, to seek Him. Now is the time. Now is the time to choose Jesus Christ, before this life runs its brief course, and eternity begins.

CHAPTER 10

No Second Thoughts

Y̶ou might have seen a clever advertisement on TV which depicts a man sneaking *incognito* into a McDonalds restaurant. Desperately seeking to hide his identity, he shelters behind some bushes, wears a disguise and steals up to the service counter only when nobody is watching. As he orders a burger, we—the viewers—are busy wondering why he is behaving this way, when the camera cuts outside to the parking lot and the truth is revealed: the sign on the side of his truck says 'Vegetarian Gourmet Food'. Yet he is tucking into a Big Mac! By eating meat, in other words, he is caught in the act of compromising his confessed loyalty to vegetarianism.

A similar syndrome faces us after we have turned from the world to follow Christ. We can be tempted to flirt again with the very things that once held us captive.

Don't look back

The Bible speaks of this issue often. For example, there is the lesson of Lot's wife. In Genesis 19, when God destroyed Sodom and Gomorrah, Lot and his family were commanded not to look back as they made their escape. Lot's wife, however, "looked back, and she became a pillar of salt" (Genesis 19:26). In the New Testament, Jesus uses this to teach his followers not to remain attached to this world: "Remember Lot's wife! Whoever tries to keep his life will lose it, and whoever loses his life will preserve it" (Luke 17:32-33).What is Jesus getting at here? He is saying that if we want to follow him, we must not keep looking back to the world with longing but look forward (or homeward) and fix our eyes on God.

On another occasion, Jesus said it this way: "No one who puts his hand to the plough and looks back is fit for service in the kingdom of God" (Luke 9:62). He said this in response to someone who claimed he wanted to follow Jesus, but first wanted to say goodbye to his family? But even this seemingly worthy cause gets short shrift from Jesus at this point, and here we gain a sharp (and startling) insight into what it means to become a disciple of Jesus. Surely following him does not require us to put our Christian faith above literally *everything else,* even house and home, even kith and kin? Apparently, it does. Jesus is saying that following him requires the same concentration and forward-looking dedication necessary to plough a field (which in those days involved an ox with a wooden implement that would quickly go off course if the farmer turned his attention away, even momentarily). Once we decide to follow Jesus, it is fatal to look back because, like the farmer who turns his head, we will no longer be going in a straight line.

What was it that Lot's wife looked back to? Answer: her old life. What is it that a farmer might turn away from his plough for? Answer: a call from the sidelines. Applied to us, we too can be distracted by the things that we worshiped before coming to Christ. The world and its loyalties have a way of continuing to act as a powerful distraction to us, especially since we have each absorbed so much of its values simply by growing up in a society that denies God. Like everyone else in contemporary Western culture, Christians have imbibed the dream of the Good Life, eaten at the table of Post-Modernism, and been infected with the virus of Secularism. These are not reversed or jettisoned overnight, but remain in our system with all their implied expectations of entitlement, individualism and self. So we need to honestly ask ourselves, those of us who are believers, am I sure it has been God I have been worshipping? Or have I been looking back over my shoulder at all the old worldly icons I supposedly left behind, be they prestige, career, comfort, fame, wealth, travel, hobbies, house, or whatever?

Backsliding

Our relationship with God is a bit like elastic, in that you can stretch it and you know that though taut, it is not broken. As born-again believers we are not yet perfect, and although the principle and power of sin have been broken in our lives, we are still tempted to flirt with the world. It is as if we take our relationship with God and stretch it, like a rubber band. As born-again believers, we do this every time we lapse into sin, but things don't quite reach breaking point. Though flirting with the world we are still–by God's grace in Christ–bound to Him. Our status with him remains intact. Yet when believers behave this way, it is disobedient and perverse, and we need to recognize it for what it is: the insidious problem of 'backsliding'.

In the letter to churches in the book of Revelation, this kind of warning is one that Jesus emphasizes to his hearers. To the church at Ephesus, he says "you have forsaken your first love; remember the height from which you have fallen;

repent and do the things you did at first" (2:4-5). If they do not regain their original love for God, Jesus continues, they are in danger of losing their status in the kingdom altogether. Jesus scolds the churches at Pergamum and Thyatira for tolerating the worldly teachings and practices of the pagan culture they have been called out from (such as sexual immorality and idol worship). To the church at Laodicea, the message is again about the danger of compromise with the world: they were trusting in their material wealth rather than God, and this made their faith "lukewarm", neither hot nor cold, and Jesus is about to "spit them out" of his mouth.

It is a subtle and ever-present problem. Like a fish in water, Christians are constantly immersed in a pagan society. We are called to live *in* the world, but not be *of* the world. There is therefore a line to be walked between engagement with our surrounding culture and separation from that culture, and as believers we continually need to ask how this is to be worked out in practice.

At one extreme is legalism (such as the arbitrary rules of a previous generation that Christians couldn't smoke, dance, go to movies or wear lipstick) or a kind of withdrawn separatism (like that of the traditional Mennonites or Amish). But these extreme approaches replace the gospel with law, effectively undermining that gospel. It amounts to a distorted degree of world-denial that is effectively anti-world. This is not consistent with the Bible, which affirms that the creation is not intrinsically evil, but good in God's sight.

At the other extreme, however, is a lazy integration with the world's values, where the Christian leads a lifestyle that amounts to little more than a kind of baptized worldliness. Too many concessions and compromises result, and the believer's faith seems indistinguishable from his unbelieving next door neighbour's lack-of-faith. Though he believes in God, such a Christian behaves as if, for all intents and purposes, human existence is limited to this earthly life. He has embraced the world in a manner that is warned against in Scripture (1 John 2:15), and is living a kind of practical atheism.

It is the second extreme which is the more clear and present danger for most believers. As an old aphorism puts it, Christians are supposed to "have the boat in the water, but not the water in the boat". Are our career choices, house in the suburbs, two-car luxury, relativistic ways of thinking, self-gratifying character traits and the like entirely surrendered to God's rule? Are we guided by what Jesus holds to be important, or do we simply accommodate ourselves to the surrounding culture? When we adopt the operating methods and priorities of the world, it dilutes the witness of the church in society. When Christians buy into the culture's way of seeing life, it becomes difficult to offer a critique of that culture as we hold out the gospel. Consequently, the role of being 'salt' and 'light' (Matthew 5:13-16) is put at risk, because the things we Christians love are no longer sufficiently distinctive or revolutionary.

Ask yourself this question: Am I desiring to feel at ease in a world that I am supposed to feel ill-at-ease in? Then we should take on board the Apostle Paul's attitude:

See to it that no one takes you captive through hollow and deceptive philosophy, which depends on human tradition and the basic principles of this world rather than on Christ (Colossians 2:8).

This means adopting the posture of conscientious scrutineer of the many things that can conflict with my loyalty to Christ, if it appears those things are getting the better of me. I will be careful to keep everything else in its place, subordinate to Him: possessions, comforts, friendships, reputation, ambitions, family, health, likes, dislikes, pleasures–even life itself. These things are certainly permissible, and even valuable in their place, but their final authority over me is denied. Jesus says to seek first the kingdom of God, and let these other things come our way at God's good pleasure. So it is a question of where we're aiming. As C. S. Lewis once put it: "Aim at heaven and you will get earth thrown in". Aim at earth, however, and you end up getting neither.

Single-minded

Being single-minded in our pursuit of God is an important theme in the Bible. The Psalmist tells God, "I seek you with all my heart" (119:10) and in another place, Scripture says, "your hearts must be fully committed to the Lord our God" (1 Kings 8:61). The New Testament echoes this, saying that Barnabas encouraged the believers to "remain true to the Lord with all their hearts" (Acts 11:23), and urging us to "set our minds on things above, not on earthly things" (Colossians 3:2).

As believers, what can happen gradually over the years is that the fire in our belly dies down till it is little more than a spark. Other things begin to creep in and the 'crowding out' effect occurs. The place of God in our lives becomes hopelessly entangled with the worldly concerns and pursuits that have somehow found their way back into our thinking. Like in the parable of the sower, thorns and thistles grow up and choke the dynamism of the gospel in our living (Luke 8:5-8). We "quench the Spirit" (1 Thessalonians 5:19) because of our worldly distractions.

Contrast this syndrome with an important strand of biblical thought in which the Scriptures talk of giving God our very best, rather than the leftovers as a kind of afterthought. This is reflected in a number of places and images in Scripture:

- *The first fruits.* In the Old Testament, when Israel harvested their produce, they were commanded to give the 'first fruits' of the soil to God as an offering (Exodus 23:19). The principle embodied here is that if we are to follow God, we should seek to give him the best of our time and resources and efforts. Today, however, we so often reverse this by putting our primary passion and energy into our home, career and family–then if there is anything 'left over' for religion we might make a token gesture to God from the dregs of our time and aspirations.

- *Gifts without blemish.* In the Old Testament system of sacrificing an animal on the altar to God, it was always a temptation to use an injured or sick one that was of lesser economic value, and hold back the good ones for taking to market. But Leviticus 22:21 says to offer only a lamb "without defect or blemish" as a sign of highest esteem for the Lord. To do otherwise is to show "contempt for God's name" (Malachi 1:6-8). Yet we are more apt to treat God with contempt by giving him our second-best effort. We settle for a lower level of enthusiasm and attention in the spiritual side of life than we apply to our finances, family, and so on.

- *Building God's house before our own.* In the Bible book of

Haggai (chapter 1), the people of Israel, upon returning to the promised land, are ordered to rebuild the temple. However, they take it upon themselves to decide that "the time has not yet come for the Lord's house to be built" and instead devote their money and effort to beautifying their own private residences. Through his prophet, God chides them, saying: "Is it a time for you yourselves to be living in your panelled houses while this house (i.e God's kingdom program) remains in a ruin?" (1:4). The principle here is that we should not put a higher priority on our own personal advancement, bigger homes, improved comfort, lower golf handicap and the like, than we put upon the things of God. For instance, why are we so diligent and meticulous when studying the designer details of new cars, but lax when it comes to studying the Bible and the truth about God? This is but one example.

Distracted to death

What happens when a 'believer' stretches the elastic band so far that it breaks? This is no longer just a matter of flirting with the world: the alleged 'believer' is in reality re-married to the world, and has fallen back into something akin to idolatry. They are not simply backslidden. The person has forfeited their relationship with God. Such a person is in a very serious situation, according to the New Testament:

> *If they have escaped the corruption of the world by knowing our Lord and Saviour Jesus Christ, and are again entangled in it and overcome, they are worse off at the end than they were at the beginning (2 Peter 2:20).*

The Bible writer goes on to say it would have been better for them not to have known the way of righteousness in the first place, than to have known it and then turn their backs on it. Then a strong picture is used, quoting Proverbs: it is like a "dog returning to its vomit". When a person has tasted the life-giving food of the gospel, in other words, going back to their old way of thinking is like eating their own vomit!

Here we see two important things. First, becoming a Christian involves expelling the values of this world from our system. It is not meant to be a 'cold conversion', where a person merely makes a nominal mental note about Jesus but the impact on them is still shallow, weak and not life-changing. Instead, Christian conversion should be deep and permanent, involving a costly break with the world. Regrettably, there are doubtless some churchgoers whose 'conversion' was not genuine, whose attachment to the world has never been severed. They are still in their sin, with no inheritance in heaven.

And then secondly, we see that some so-called converts, having claimed a turning away to Christ, then return to the values of the dying world, like a dog to its vomit. Like a "sow that is washed and goes back to her wallowing in the mud", as the Bible writer next describes it (2 Peter 2:22). This too is a striking image, of a person who at first believes in Jesus but whose love of the world proves too much and they return to wallow in their old passions. Instead of hanging loose to worldly ways, and taking firm hold of the salvation Jesus offers from death and hell, many persist in being obsessed with trivialities—like whether their car is prestigious or not, whether someone they know lives in a nicer suburb than they do, whether the furnishings in the living room are colour coordinated like in *Vogue* magazine, and so on. If the truth be known, they serve such things instead of God. Their Christianity is effectively still-born. They have not been born again.

When a person retains a primary love of the world above God, the elastic has snapped. They are no longer reconciled to God (if they ever were) and it is appropriate to invoke the biblical concept of *idolatry*.

What is the nature of idols? Idols are dead. This is one of the most important things the Bible says about them. The episode of Elijah and the prophets of Baal (1 Kings 18:16-46) epitomizes this point. Israel had forsaken the true God and was following Baal and Asherah, two foreign deities. So Elijah challenges the Israelites: "How long will you waver between two opinions? If the Lord is God, follow him; if Baal is God, follow him." The people said nothing. So Elijah had two bulls brought and placed on two altars, as a test. He challenged the priests of Baal to "call on the name of your god" to bring down fire, and they called from morning until evening but nothing happened. Not a spark appeared on their bull, not a flame on their altar.

Then it was Elijah's turn. To make the demonstration doubly convincing, he asked that water be poured over the offering and the wood, soaking it through. Three times they soaked it. Next he prayed a simple prayer to God. Then "the fire of the Lord" fell and burned up the sacrifice, the wood, the stones and the soil, and also dried up all the water. And when all the people saw this, they fell down and cried: "The Lord—he is God!".

Idols cannot save. Isaiah writes that an idol is simply something man-made (Isaiah 40:19), and points out how ridiculous it is for a living human being to be captivated by an object (44:15-17). Of what value is an idol, asks Habakkuk (2:18)? For we know that an idol is nothing at all (1 Corinthians 8:4). An idol can be a tangible object, but it need not be, as outlined in chapter 2. Our "desires and greed" are idolatry too (Colossians 3:5, Ephesians 5:5). This makes the danger all-embracing, because clearly we can be greedy or obsessive about a whole host of things, from fame and fortune right through to privacy and housekeeping.

The Bible makes clear the command of God to people who like to call themselves Christians but are still in idolatry: "do not love the world or anything in the world" (1 John 2:15), for this world is passing away. You and I need to wake up and smell the coffee. It is not enough to say we believe in God. We believe in many things, from clean air to Captain Cook, but belief at this level proves very little. Nor is it even enough to have a 'deeply-held' belief in God, for when the time comes to put it to the test it may be seen to run second to another, more deeply held conviction. No, the Bible goes a step further again, and makes the outrageous and seemingly unreasonable demand that God must be *our most deeply held belief,* second to nothing and no-one else in life.

The way forward

For a genuine believer who has backslidden, whose first love for God has dimmed, all is not lost. The way forward is to embrace afresh the great truth of the gospel, to be reminded again of all God has done for them in Christ Jesus.

Remember what we were before God shone his light in our life: we were lost, on the road to hell, and under the judgment of God. Outside Christ, we were each condemned and dead in our sin (Ephesians 2:1-3). Yet by the death of

Jesus on the cross, we received forgiveness, we were shown mercy. Through no merit of our own, we received the grace of God in the form of a divine pardon, and knew for the first time the deep love of God. How wonderful! How astonishing was that moment, when we understood Christ had washed away our sin, that our transgressions had been dealt with, and that God had turned us from enemies into friends. The promise of God was given, that he would never desert us or leave us and that nothing could separate us from him (Romans 8:39). We knew the meaning of divine mercy.

What is this mercy? It is when you do not receive the punishment you deserve, like an amnesty for corrupt police or the reprieve of a prisoner on death row. What is this grace? It means to be given a good gift when you did not earn it. Why did you and I receive grace and mercy from God? Because of the sacrificial death of Jesus on the cross in our place. And what should we do in response? Embrace it. Embrace afresh this love God offers, by believing the truth that we have already been told, the truth that God has revealed that can make a man wise for salvation. And what is this truth? It is Jesus Christ himself, as revealed in the Scriptures, who by grace brings salvation to all those who put their trust in him.

It's useful to recall from history the story of the Spanish explorer Cortez, who conquered Mexico. At the prospect of the invasion, his troops were fearful, and so upon landing, Cortez burned all his ships in the harbour. He left them in no doubt—there was no way back. The only way open to them was forward. And in a similar way, when we call ourselves 'believers', we too need to close off all return routes to our old life. We need to be clear in our minds that there is no turning back.

The gospel is the antidote to the backsliding believer, for as that well-known hymn puts it, when you turn your eyes upon Jesus and look full in his wonderful face, then the things of earth will grow strangely dim—in the light of his glory and grace.

New Priorities

When we have turned from love of the world, to love of God, what implications does it have for our goals and aims in life?

One of the oldest pranks known to young boys involves visiting a leading department store and switching the price tags on various goods. For maximum effect, it is always best to swap tags on two items of widely different value– and then sit back and chuckle at the faces of confused customers, who are totally bamboozled by the junkie trinkets carrying exorbitant price tags, and the expensive goods marked at absurdly low rates.

When we place a high value on the fleeting issues and earthly preoccupations of the world, and correspondingly devalue the eternal agenda of God, this is what we are doing: switching the price tags. And one of the first things involved in following Jesus is to let him put the price tags right again, because left to our own devices we tend to undervalue the important and overvalue the unimportant things in life.

Who sets the agenda?

The first issue involves setting our life agenda. Suppose we say to ourselves something like: "I know God wants to be involved in my life. So I will look to him in all I am doing. For example, in every part of my timetable–whether it be my family, my music, my work–I will look up what the Bible says about these subjects and frame my involvement in each of these activities with a biblical rationale." Then we will be putting God number one in our life, right?

Wrong. We are still not letting God be in charge, and you know why? We are not letting him *set our agenda*. Although we may be willing to let him help us work through our agenda, it is still *our* agenda and not *his*. We are not allowing him to shape where that agenda came from in the first place. We are falling into a form of world-love which worships our own small program ahead of God's big one. In effect, we are imposing our questions on God's answers.

It is vital to realise that we are all amazingly self-centred.

There is a story about a leading Scottish newspaper that reported the sinking of the Titanic under the parochial head-line: "GLASGOW MAN LOST AT SEA"! The tragedy of the hundreds of people from many nations who lost their lives was subsumed under the extremely minor point that one of the victims happened to be from the readers' home town!

We each tend to view the world through the lens of home-interest and me-importance. We are deeply self-referencing, says the Bible, and in keeping with this character flaw we attach incorrect weights to the various items in our lives, twisting their true importance out of proportion. It is like we take God's perfect agenda for life, and hold it up to one of those curved fun mirrors that they have in amusement parks, resulting in a distorted human version.

This syndrome lies behind much of our questioning of God. For instance, as I travel around speaking to people about Christ, they often say: "It's all very well to talk about Jesus, but why doesn't he show himself to me—then I will believe. If only he would make a grand entrance somewhere, or appear before the assembled media of the world, it could put an end to speculation about God, once and for all". However, this is a severe case of trying to set the agenda instead of letting God do it himself. The fact is, Jesus has *already* made the grand entrance, done more miracles than you could poke a stick at, and had the biggest impact on human history of anyone. It just wasn't in our century—how humiliating! Someone else got the front row seats. Our irritation is that God chose to send Jesus in the first century, not the twentieth. It is not our place to alter that, yet in our self-centredness, we naturally like to think that we should be the centre of attention, that our century should have been the chosen one, that our city deserves the privilege of direct visual proof of Jesus (and that we should not be expected to believe simply on the basis of eyewitness testimony from back then). But the hard fact is, our time and place is not as special as we wish it was.

Let me say that again: our personal agendas are not as important as we like to think they are. They are worldly. They come from Wall Street, Fleet Street or the High Street. Each year *Cleo* magazine runs a contest for the most eligible bachelors around town, and the four criteria used are: Personality, Power, Profile and Presentation. Why these ones? Because this is what their readers are fascinated by; it is what the public believes in and hankers after. And if we are honest, these are what we hanker after too, in our secret desires. In our hearts, we want these four things, and so we pursue them in our lives. They become our main agenda. Robert Reich, former US Secretary of Labor, astutely remarked recently that while "the ancients worried about the moods of the skies, mountains, seas and forests", we moderns are "placating a pavement", meaning Wall Street. He was bemoaning the overwhelming influence of the economic agenda on our lives. And it even affects our approach to God: books are written on 'Success through Faith' and 'Prosperity through Prayer', implying that God is there to help us meet our worldly goals. He is not.

TV shows such as *Seinfeld* help us to see ourselves in the mirror, just like *Leave it to Beaver* did back in the 1950s. And as we look at the characters in *Seinfeld* and others like it, the warning lights should go on.

The characters are essentially unspiritual and self-absorbed people. That's why we love them. They're like us, or like we would be if only we had the nerve. Their lives revolve around obsessions like eating, money, casual sex, and worrying about what other people think of them. As critic David Dale wrote recently, they are typical residents of your neighbourhood or mine: George got himself engaged to a girl he didn't love then wished her dead so he could get out of the relationship; Elaine is a self-deluding neurotic who is obsessed with getting people into bed; Cosmo uses his eccentricity to exploit others; while Jerry is a compulsive womaniser who gargles six times a day.

These fictional characters bear out an important truth about ourselves: that our agendas are governed by trivial urban fictions. For example, here's a test: whose job would you say is more significant, the school principal or the school scripture teacher? Our instinct is to say that the headmaster's job is more important, but in fact in God's eyes it is the other way around. The headmaster is simply keeping the 'back office' running; the scripture teacher is doing the fundamental kingdom work of advancing Christianity.

Much of our daily existence is captive to our own agendas that we falsely turn into life-or-death issues. We attach far too much gravity to the trivial, and give much too little weight to the things of God. We commit the theological equivalent of putting the immediate ahead of the important. We switch the price tags.

The priorities of Jesus

Jesus combats this way of thinking in no uncertain terms. According to him, there is absolutely no room for argument: God's kingdom is the primary agenda that matters most. Full stop. End of discussion. All other agendas represent false quasi-idols.

He explains this by likening the kingdom of God to a merchant looking for fine pearls (Matthew 13:45-46). When he found one of great value, he went away and sold everything he had to buy it—not just selling his pearls, but all his other possessions as well. Notice the expensive nature of the swap: to gain the kingdom, the man knew it was worth giving up everything else. For 'everything else' is the price of gaining heaven. So precious is Christian salvation that it is priceless.

What is Jesus up to here? He is putting right the price tags again, price tags that we wrongly switched, by showing that our earthly obsessions are in the end worth little, while the eternal things of God are worth much. This is the unique situation involved in following Christ, where we too must act like the merchant who greatly values the perfect pearl. We must be willing to discount all our habitual human prizes—ones that we have been conditioned to treat as highly desirable through many years of subliminal messages from our culture. We must discount them in comparison to the one prize that really matters: the future 'crown of life' that awaits us when we commit to Christ (James 1:12). Conversion to Christ always involves a radical re-ordering of life's priorities and values.

How, in practice, do we implement this at the level of life's agenda? By switching from our own personal program to God's kingdom program, and allowing it to shape our priorities.

What is God's program? He is moulding us to be like Jesus. He is building his church (Matthew 16:18), making disciples of Christ (Matthew 28:19), by spreading his word (Acts 6:7). God is in the sole business of saving souls for eternity, and remaking us into his likeness. This is his 'core business'; indeed, it is his only business. And he never gets sidetracked from it: he always 'sticks to the knitting' as the old expression goes. In fact, the way God sees things, only two remaining stages are still to happen in human history:

And this gospel of the kingdom will be preached in the whole world as a testimony to all nations, and then the end will come (Matthew 24:14).

In God's scheme of things, first the gospel will be spread to all parts of planet earth; then Jesus will return to wrap things up. Closing time. The end of history. The start of eternity.

Given that this gospel enterprise is God's big agenda, then where does that leave everything else in life? It's just housekeeping. That's all it is. Everything else, no matter how impressive—the US war machine, the Olympic Games, Nobel prize-winning discoveries, famous works of art, our careers, great nights out, our achievements, our assets, protection of the environment—all of it is a mere sideshow to the main attraction, which is God building his church.

This does not mean these other things are 'bad', or that we must rule them out of our experience altogether. That is the opposite error, of monasticism. But what it *does* mean is that they must not be allowed to drive our agenda. We must hang loose to them all, and hold tenaciously only to the program of Jesus Christ. All those other things are to be treated as extras that may—or may not—come our way. The only necessity on our timetable should be the kingdom of God, in our own life and the lives of others.

It follows that we need to see life through the new 'grid' of Jesus' kingdom. Let me illustrate. Soldiers in the world's best equipped armies today wear a small flip-down video screen on their battle helmets. It folds down in front of their eyes and gives a live feed using satellite signals, showing a grid map of the strategic layout of the area in front of them. The purpose is to sift out, from all the many terrain features in view, those which are important to their primary mission. We need to wear the theological equivalent, by looking at the world through the grid of kingdom-priorities. The Bible is our 'map', and society is our 'terrain'. When we do this, we will begin to alter our life agenda so that it fits with the prime directive of knowing Christ and making him known. We will soon treat ordinary things as options and kingdom things as essentials, because we will value above all else the pearl of great price.

This brings us to a crucial principle for living the Christ-centred life. It is not enough to have a faith that is 'Bible-based'. Our faith must be Bible-*driven*. Let me explain. If we are to allow God to set the agenda, then *getting our questions from the Bible is just as important as getting our answers from the Bible.*

If we approach the Bible with a predetermined emphasis, with our own list of issues, we will almost certainly come to the wrong conclusions. When we say we 'believe the Bible', this must include deciding which aspects of our life will be ranked as important, and which ones unimportant, even if it means discovering that our own set of pet interests are simply not high on God's agenda, interests like:

- how can I succeed in my business or career?
- how can we make the trains run on time?
- how does the new Holden compare with the new Ford?
- is rugby union better than rugby league?
- what colour should we paint our living room?

These and similar questions receive a lot of attention in our lives, but when we come to the Bible, we find it is largely silent about such issues. This silence in itself is very, very significant: the Bible teaches us much by what it does *not* say, as well as by what it does say. When the Bible is silent on an issue, this is giving us the important clue that the issue does not figure in God's central priorities. And nor should it in ours.

We can respond to this dilemma in one of two ways. One is to do what many people do, and refuse to concede that our own personal list of priorities is secondary in the overall scheme of things. Many people either try to get God to say something about it through superstitious means (such as astrology or charismatic utterances), or else give up listening to God at all, and just get on with their own pet agenda in life without him (often unaware of the terrible consequences down the track).

The other response is to acknowledge the Bible's message that, left to ourselves, we all tend to be side-tracked by minor questions, and begin to shape our life around a new set of questions, those that are central to the pages of Scripture, questions like:

- who made us and has the right to our worship?
- who is Jesus Christ and what did he come to do?
- what is God's central project on this planet?
- what is God's ideal for families and churches?
- how can I be part of God's kingdom and work?
- what sort of character does God want me to develop?

These are the core questions in the Bible. They dominate its pages, from Genesis to Revelation, and they sum up the agenda of God. This is the 'grid' that we need to flip down in front of our field of vision in order that we might understand what it is in our lives that ranks uppermost in the mind of God.

The challenge is, am I willing to make His agenda my agenda? Am I willing to submit to the Bible's ranking of priorities?

In the movie *Groundhog Day*, starring Bill Murray and Andie McDowell, a man has to re-live the same day over and over again until he learns the purpose of his life. Before he is allowed to proceed any further through his years, he must first learn to approach life in its proper context, by practising a single day many times until the penny drops. At the beginning of the film he is a cynical, self-absorbed character who sees everything in terms of how it affects him, but by the end of the whole experience he is a different person: considerate, aware of others, and no longer obsessed with himself. His whole agenda is different. He has had a kind of conversion.

Switching to God's agenda is like that. Instead of imposing our own set of questions on the Bible, we will let the Bible impose its questions on us. Instead of weighting God and the things in my life by my own assessment, I will allow the Bible to determine the relative weighting for me. In short, I will let God set the agenda.

The method of Jesus

We have been talking above about a Type 1 error: imposing our questions on God's answers. Now we turn to consider a Type 2 error: imposing our answers on God's questions.

This is the subtle mistake we often make of embracing God's agenda, only to then try to implement it by using our own techniques instead of his. This happens when we have noble ends but use unsanctioned means to achieve them, when we have Christian goals but use a sub-Christian *modus operandi* in pursuit of those goals. It amounts to a subtle form of world-love.

One of the most famous works of art in the world is an etching from the late nineteenth century by Edward Munch entitled *The Scream*. It depicts, in dreary black and white, a shadowy landscape, in which the central figure is screaming. The subject has their hands over their ears and wears a wraith-like appearance, with their mouth open, howling. Yet it is a silent scream, for we cannot hear a painting. The figure represents humanity at large, and the unmistakable message from the artist is that human existence is essentially one of despair and loneliness, with the terror that nobody hears the inner silent scream of the soul. In the face of suffering, life is a seemingly pointless and tortuous experience, and the world is a desolation.

It strikes a chord. As thinking people, we cannot help but feel the weight of human tragedy in our world today. Many problems still exist, despite centuries of apparent progress. Hunger. Rape. War. Injustice. Greed. Environmental degradation. Racism. Sexism. Oppression. Consumerism. Inequality. Exploitation. Apathy. Crime. Urban decay. Poverty. Division. Divorce. Drugs. Unemployment. And in our personal lives we experience all too frequently the ripple effects of society's problems on our families, friends and communities.

Something must be done about all this, we agree. Like Martin Luther King, we have a dream, a dream of a world without divisions of race, divisions of gender, divisions of having and not having. We all agree that something must be done to fix our economic problems, repair the family, regain law and order, raise moral standards, not to mention other problems like ecology, equality, world peace, minority rights and the like.

So we set up social justice programs and attempt cultural engineering projects to address it all. The philosophy is irresistible: if we can work together, join hands and strive for a better world, we can 'return to Eden', to an idyllic existence without want, without injustice, without war. We valiantly teach our school children to have high ideals for tomorrow, to seek unity and harmony. And as adults we too have our own rituals for voicing such grand hopes, like the Olympic Games, where at least for a short while all races and creeds can be united around a single purpose and celebrate our common bond. Or the United Nations, which holds International Years for various causes, such as Peace and the Family.

The weight of such noble hopes is increased when we notice that God too seems to share our concerns. Even a casual reading of the Bible soon reminds us that the kingdom of God is somehow bound up with healing the deep scars that afflict humanity. In the Scriptures there is talk of restoring economic justice (Exodus 23:6), bringing peace among nations (Zechariah 9:10), loving our neighbour (Romans 13:10), caring for the environment (Genesis 2:15), finding unity (John 17:23), an end to greed (Proverbs 15:27), and so on.

Yes, it is true, the God of the Bible is deeply concerned with many of the same problems we worry about for our families and our future. And so, we reason, God must want us to be repairing our neighbourhood for the better, and it would seem to follow logically that God wants us to target our energies on the commonly accepted tools of reform, in particular:

- counselling centres
- educating our children to be model citizens
- political and parliamentary processes
- courses in ethics for business and law
- campaigning for social justice
- nation-building
- global forums such as the United Nations
- community support networks such as Parents and Citizens
- environmental groups such as Greenpeace
- service clubs like Rotary and Lions
- moral instruction for our families
- economic planning

Right? Wrong. We need to pause a minute. Something is

not adding up. Our casual reading of the Bible was just that: a little too casual. Although the list above sounds compelling, in fact we need to back up a step.

The problem is that these solutions leave God out. They may aim at the right ends, but they represent the wrong means. The response of modern mankind is to combine human resources–medical, economic, political and cybernetic–in a united effort to engineer solutions. I put it to you that *primary* reliance on the methods listed above, as helpful as they are, in fact represents a serious departure from the central remedy in the Bible, which is the gospel of God. They amount to an alternative kingdom, a man-made kingdom, a form of worldly idolatry. Although notionally addressed to the concerns that we find in the Bible, they are far removed from the real *solution* that we find in the Bible: namely, the spread of the gospel of Jesus Christ.

Put simply, God's ordained method for fixing our broken world is to start by fixing our broken lives, and he does it using 'old time religion', where the message of Jesus' death and resurrection is advertised and embraced. It is a radical solution, and not what we instinctively expect. Outrageous really. Just Jesus and preaching. Mere words. It seems hopelessly impractical, even pathetic. To men and women of practical mind, used to getting things done and getting it done their way, it seems an absurd response to the great problems that threaten to overwhelm us in the world today. Yet it is the method of God, the technique by which He is putting right everything that is wrong with us and our planet.

Why don't we like this method? Why do we find it so tempting to try our own remedies? We don't like it because it humbles us. The crux of all human methods of social engineering is to trust in our own strength, while the gospel method forces us to put our trust in God. This presents a hurdle. It is somewhat humiliating for us to rely solely on God's revealed method, because it implies that God has all the power and we have none. The Bible's prescription is annoying and unpalatable: it contradicts all the social idealists of human history, by saying that humanitarian programs are never going to fully succeed, and that man-made efforts to create unity are flawed. Only by preaching the gospel of Christ, and waiting upon God, will lasting reform come.

The episode of the Tower of Babel is instructive here (in Genesis chapter 11). After the great flood in which God rescued Noah and his family, mankind had the opportunity to make a fresh start. The whole world had one language and a common speech, and conditions seemed perfect for humanity to get it right this time and not repeat the mistakes of Adam and Eve. Except for one fact: humans are sinful. The people all said to each other, "Come, let's make bricks and bake them thoroughly. Let us build ourselves a city, with a tower that reaches to the heavens, so that we may make a name for ourselves and not be scattered over the face of the earth." But the Lord God came down to see the city and the tower that the men were building. The Lord said, "If as one people speaking the same language they have begun to do this, then nothing they plan to do will be impossible for them. Come, let us go down and confuse their language so they will not understand each other."

So we read that the Lord scattered them from there all over the earth, and they stopped building the city. That is why it is called Babel (which is a pun on the Hebrew word for 'confused') because God confused the language of the whole world.

The crucial phrases are "make a name for ourselves" and "reach to the heavens". What was going on in their minds as they built the tower, with their impressive brick-making and skyscraper technology? In effect, they were challenging God in the same way Adam and Eve did back at the beginning, trying to dispense with God, trying to take heaven by storm. It failed. God thwarted their effort, deliberately dividing them and confusing their language.

Does that come as a surprise? That God deliberately makes for division? Isn't God supposedly in favour of harmony and peace? It might seem counter-intuitive, but clearly God does not aim for unity for its own sake. And nor should we. For before Christianity provides a bridge that connects, it is first a canal that divides. Jesus said: "I have not come to bring peace, but a sword" (Matthew 10:34), making clear that it is not unity by any means, but only unity by the gospel of Christ that is sanctioned and worth pursuing. This alone is the true and lasting unity, and we know from the Bible that this kind of unity comes only through an explicit connection through Jesus Christ, not just any community network or social structure. The mandate we have been given is a very specific one: to build a new world by the gospel alone; nothing more and nothing less.

The closer we look at the biographies of Jesus in the New Testament, the clearer it becomes. The primary method of Jesus of Nazareth for changing the world in his earthly ministry was to tell of the kingdom of God. This is made clear from the start, when he tells his disciples: "Let us go somewhere else, to the nearby villages, so I can preach there also. That is why I have come" (Mark 1:38). He turns his back on distractions so that he can devote himself to his true mission.

Beyond band-aid solutions

Humanism fails because it treats the symptoms, but not the underlying disease. The Christian gospel succeeds because it directly prescribes the remedy for the disease itself: sin. Humanistic methods achieve only reform, and so are not radical enough. The gospel of Jesus Christ, by contrast, achieves revolution and so changes the heart of the person at its core. What then do humanist solutions amount to in the end? Little more than window-dressing. The wrong box of tools. The real problem in our world is our relationship with God, and unless this is addressed then nothing has fundamentally changed.

Don't get me wrong: there is certainly some value in community, political and welfare programs. Indeed, Christians do well to give support to them. The Bible itself urges us simply to "do good to all people" as we have opportunity. But the trouble with taking our philosophies of social engineering too far is that, because they look in some way similar to the concerns of Christianity, it is easy to mistake them for the real thing. For instance, many feel that educating their kids in their rights and responsibilities as citizens is just as good as sending them to Sunday School. But the two are quite different: one brings them into personal relationship with Jesus, the other does not. It is like trying to become Christian by standing on the spot a Christian just stood a moment ago, or like trying to become tall by standing next to a tall person. I may wish I was over six feet tall, but no amount of standing next to someone who is over six feet will make me that. And in the same way, teaching my children the ethics of Jesus is not the same as proclaiming to them forgiveness of sins by the cross of Jesus.

There is one sure way to tell the difference between

human methods and God's. The gospel solution is *eschatological:* that is, it is about the future. Although we catch a small glimpse of God's new world now when we become Christians, the complete fulfillment of God's program will not happen until Jesus returns. It is absolutely beyond doubt that one day God will fix the world once and for all, that he will put everything back where it belongs, that he will right all the wrongs (for a wonderful description of paradise under God, see Amos 9:13-15 and Revelation 21:1-5). All the same, it cannot happen yet. We cannot engineer it now, but rather must wait upon God. To attempt to establish paradise prematurely, by human effort and methods, is a Type 2 error. Only when Jesus returns will the kingdom of God be fully consummated.

Unless the Lord builds the house, its builders labour in vain (Psalm 127:1). So here's the question: is my life shaped around God's great mission to the world? Is his agenda of building his church my central agenda too? And in working for a better world, am I giving priority to his method—of spreading the gospel of Jesus—over human methods that have their origin in the world?

CHAPTER 12

New Relationships

The great Dutch artist Rembrandt mostly painted portraits of people, but sometimes he turned his hand to landscapes. One such picture that sticks in my mind is his *Landscape with a Stone Bridge*, painted in 1638. A river divides the picture in two, with a stone bridge connecting one side of the river with the other. It shows a man crossing the bridge from left to right, leaving behind a public inn (which the artist uses to symbolise 'the world'), and heading for the opposite side. We might think of the bridge as symbolising Christ, the one who paves the way for sinners to cross over to God.

Pictured on the other side is a village church. This image, complete with stones and steeple, is the symbol Rembrandt uses to represent the traveller's new destination: the kingdom of God. It's an apt one, because when God calls us in the gospel to *detach* ourselves from love of self that the world represents, the flipside is his call to *attach* ourselves to others, especially the redeemed people of God.

From servitude to servanthood

Once we come to understand and believe the gospel, and decide to follow Jesus, our lives are meant to take on a whole new orientation. Instead of living for self, we now live for God. The New Testament rings with this idea:

> *And he died for all, that those who live should no longer*
> *live for themselves but for him who died for them and was*
> *raised again (2 Corinthians 5:15).*

Since Jesus has liberated us from sin and death, in other words, we are now free to give up living selfishly and to instead live for God. And importantly, this in turn means obeying his command to love others:

> *This is the message you heard from the beginning: we*
> *should love one another (1 John 3:11).*

In fact, there is always a close connection in Scripture between embracing God in the gospel and living a life of loving others. Jesus coupled them together when summing up all the law and the prophets in Matthew chapter 22:

> *Love the Lord your God with all your heart and with*
> *all your soul and with all your mind. This is the first*
> *and greatest commandment. And the second is like it:*
> *Love your neighbour as yourself (verses 37-39).*

Later in the New Testament, in one of the most important sections on this subject, John also links together our response to God in his Son and the imperative to love:

> *And this is his command: to believe in the name of*
> *his Son, Jesus Christ, and to love one another as he*
> *commanded us (1 John 3:23).*

The message is unmistakable: like hand and glove, believing as a Christian believes, and loving as a Christian loves, go together.

Now we can put everything discussed in earlier chapters

of this book into this overall perspective: when we turn from loving the world, in effect we are turning from love of self. We are abandoning that old attitude which put ourselves at the centre and regarded everybody else as revolving around us, which was epitomised in the motto 'Me first. Me second. And Me third'. In its place, we have adopted a new philosophy which says, in effect, 'God first. Others second. Myself last'.

God's call is to live out our salvation by seeking to love others. But what *is* love? What does it look like? One thing's for sure, it is not just sentimentality or mere chemistry. Love is an action—an intentional action on our part which seeks the best interest of the other party, where that best interest is as defined by God. Often, love will not even seek what the other person thinks they 'want', but rather what they truly need, because God's purposes for people are often not what they themselves are chasing at the time. We can even love others without actually being with them in person, as the Philippian church did when sending aid to the Apostle Paul (Philippians 4:14-19), and indeed as the Lord Jesus himself demonstrated in dying on the cross for us:

> *This is how we know what love is: Jesus Christ laid down his life for us (1 John 3:16).*

The original model and supreme example of love is Jesus himself, who gave his life for us while we were still sinners, still wrapped up in ourselves and in no mind to seek him. We were not searching for God; he was not what we 'wanted'. But he was what we desperately needed. This is how God himself has showed his love for us: while we were yet sinners, Christ died for us (Romans 5:8). Hence Jesus remarked that greater love has no man than this: that he lay down his life for his friends (John 15:13).

The expectation is that we will imitate Christ by seeking the good of others. Does this new model lifestyle sound burdensome? Is the command to love others nothing more than a new kind of humiliating slavery? No. Here we need to distinguish between 'servitude' and *servanthood*. Before becoming a Christian, we were slaves to whatever worldly passions dominated us (Romans 6:16). Ultimately this led to sin and death. We could not help ourselves. We were captive even though we told ourselves we were free agents charting our own course. The Bible says we were in slavery to "the basic principles of this world" (Galatians 4:3). And it's true isn't it? Think about it: before knowing Christ, a person works their guts out trying to keep up with the Joneses, constantly wonders why their relationships keep going sour, and is forever running on a treadmill of serving the god of self-centredness that promises much but fails to deliver.

By contrast, after deciding to believe the gospel, we enter a new and different kind of 'slavery', a voluntary indenture to Christ. It is not as convicts but as free men and women that we now serve, like an olympic athlete who gladly toils to bring glory to his homeland. To serve Jesus by choice, not to earn 'brownie points', but simply as a response of sheer thankfulness for all he has won for us, is therefore most unlike slavery to the world. Paradoxically, his service is perfect freedom. The truth of the gospel, the Bible says, sets us free (John 8:32), and when the Son of God sets us free we are "free indeed" (8:36).

There is a certain kind of wonderful liberty in at last discovering the life you were meant for, like a ship that after many months of dry dock finally is berthed in water, or a train that has spent a long time confined to the engineering shed on hoists at long last being placed onto the tracks. At face value, the tracks restrict the train, but we know that only by following the tracks can the train know true freedom. For here is its design and purpose. In the same way, you and I only know proper freedom when we commit ourselves to the path God has designed for us: to believe in his Son and to live out the agenda of loving others.

Believing means belonging

The arena where this new lifestyle is played out most clearly is God's 'church'. By this is not meant the building, or a denomination, or even a particular type of meeting such as a Sunday service. Instead, we are talking about the people of God, the community of those who have been saved by believing in the gospel of Jesus Christ. Church is the network of Christ-followers, a new society brought into existence by God through the instrument of his gospel and by the continuing sustenance of that gospel.

Christianity, therefore, is not a private religion. It can never be that. As pointed out in chapter 9, in the Bible believing always implies belonging: when we enter the kingdom of God through accepting Jesus as Lord and Saviour, it carries the implication that we have joined the fellowship of God. The Bible uses a range of metaphors to capture this 'connectedness' with other believers:

- *a body:* just as each of us has one body with many parts, and these parts do not all have the same function, so in Christ we who are many form one body and each member belongs to all the others (Romans 12:4-5). We are all members of one body (Ephesians 4:25) and this is what the Bible means by God's 'church' (Colossians 1:24). We have been baptised by one Spirit into one body (1 Corinthians 12:13) and so need each other, like the eye needs the hand and *vice versa.*

- *a family:* Christians are in a familial relationship with each other, since we have all been adopted as sons or daughters by God, and are able to call him 'Father' (Romans 8:15; Matthew 6:9). The church is referred to as the "household" of God (Ephesians 2:19; 1 Timothy 3:15), and Christians are directed to treat fellow-believers as they would their own family, treating older men as fathers, younger men as brothers, older women as mothers and younger women as sisters (1 Timothy 5:1-2). The kind of love we show is frequently termed 'brotherly': we are to be devoted to other Christians in brotherly love (Romans 12:10).

- *an army:* believers are linked together in a battle against sin, the world and the devil, and are pictured using soldier imagery, being urged to "put on the full armour of God" (Ephesians 6:11). The Apostle Paul writes that Timothy should "endure hardship, like a good soldier of Christ Jesus", and that soldiers do not get distracted by civilian affairs but seek to "please their commanding officer" (2 Timothy 2:3-4). We are to fight the good fight of faith (1 Timothy 6:12) using weapons that are "not of this world" (2 Corinthians 10:4). So, as in the old hymn *Onward Christian Soldiers,* there is the sense of camaraderie involved in standing alongside others in the faith.

- *a flock:* God is pictured as the Shepherd (Psalm 23:1) who gathers together and protects his people, watching over them. In turn, believers together are like the shepherd's flock (Psalm 95:7) who are meant to be together, not scattered (Jeremiah 10:21). As there is only one shepherd, there can be only "one flock" (John 10:16). Jesus is spoken of in the Bible as the Chief Shepherd (1 Peter 5:4) and the Good Shepherd (John 10:14), whom we follow together.

- *a nation:* God's people, who have been called out according to his great purposes in Christ, effectively form a new nation under Christ. Way back near the start of the Bible's epic saga of salvation history, this was an important element of God's promise to Abraham: "I will make you into a great nation" (Genesis 12:2). As inheritors of this promise through Christ, Christians are part of this great nation of God. It is a nation that cuts across racial and cultural lines (Galatians 3:28) because God is calling people out of every society and background to be part of his eternal plan (Isaiah 66:18).

This list is not an exhaustive one, but it gives us a pretty good idea of the main point, which is that the Christian faith has an essential *corporate* thread running through it. Often, the language used in the Bible is plural rather than singular when it is addressing us about this or that aspect of the Christian lifestyle. The upshot is that, just as we spoke of above in connection to the Rembrandt picture, Christian conversion involves not only turning *away from* the world but equally turning *to* the community of God in fellowship and brotherly love with other believers. Rather than the worldly individualism we have grown up with, the secular autonomy that our society has taught us, we will need to gradually 'unlearn' it and replace it with a deep sense of belonging to fellow followers of Christ.

In place of the world and its idolatrous distractions,

upon becoming a Christian there is a new goal in life: to lay down our lives for others as part of our response to God who has rescued us.

This is patterned on the character of God himself, who is Trinity. At the heart of reality lies this magnificent biblical doctrine that God is one God in three Persons: God the Father, God the Son, and God the Holy Spirit. This great truth is unique to Christianity, and both sides of it run through Scripture in parallel. The *unity* of the Godhead is seen by both the Old Testament which affirms that "the Lord our God is one" (Deuteronomy 6:4) and the New Testament which speaks of "one God" (Ephesians 4:6). At the same time, Scripture affirms the *diversity* of God as three distinct Persons, namely "the Father, the Son and the Holy Spirit" (Matthew 28:19). We have a picture of a united Godhead that is truly plural in its membership.

The trinity tells us that reality is about relationship. In the gospel, God is calling us into a renewed set of relationships–with himself and with others–modelled on the same pattern of mutual submission and other-person-centred love found amongst the three persons of the Trinity. This is what life is all about, and is reflected in the many 'one-another' commands of Scripture: to love one another (1 Peter 4:8), to bear one another's burdens (Galatians 6:2), to submit to one another (Ephesians 5:21), to be openhanded toward one another (Deuteronomy 15:11), to encourage one another (1 Thessalonians 4:18), to serve one another (Galatians 5:13), to provide for one another (1 Timothy 5:8), to accept one another (Romans 15:7), to admonish one another (Colossians 3:16), to build one another up (Ephesians 4:29), to speak the truth to one another (Ephesians 4:15), and so on. In practical application, this agenda of serving others will have many facets, from helping the poor to fostering fellow-ship, through to contributing to the spread of the gospel. This last one is vital. We will love others enough to go out of our way to help them hear the gospel, to come to Christ and to grow in their relationship with God. This is the natural outcome of a life lived in service of others.

Marching to a different drum

What a different and revolutionary revision of our goals in life the Christian gospel holds out to us, in contrast to the dying world around us. Loving God and loving others, when patterned on the Trinity and pursued with our whole heart, will give us so much to think about and throw ourselves into, we will have less and less time for the world and its empty merry-go-round. We need to stop being mesmerized by the mundane, and rediscover the glory of God and his gospel. It's as if for too long we have had a marble (the world) right in front of our eyeball, blocking our vision. All we could see was the marble. But if we dare to move it away, a whole new landscape (God's kingdom) opens up to us, and we can see God's full scheme for life in all its splendour.

We must allow our lives to be disturbed by the gospel of Jesus Christ. This present world and its desires are passing away, but whoever does the will of God will live forever (1 John 2:17). It is a call to become deeply suspicious of our culture and its trappings, to no longer be seduced by the world, to turn away from love of false God-substitutes. In its place, there is the call to give our hearts to God, through his Son Christ Jesus. It is captured in a well-known hymn, which we have quoted as our 'theme song' several times:

Turn your eyes upon Jesus
look full in his wonderful face
and the things of earth will grow strangely dim
in the light of his glory and grace

When I give my heart to him, the rest of me will follow; when I seek first the kingdom of God, all those other good things in life will find their proper place. Yet for this to happen, there must be no rival to God in my heart of hearts. No rival to God in my affections, in my goals, in my thinking, in my living. It is a call to surrender my will to him, surrender my lesser loves to him, surrender my all to him. It is a call to march to the beat of a different drum. It is a call to turn from false and lifeless 'idols' to serve the true and living God.

About Matthias Media

Ever since 'St Matthias Press and Tapes' first opened its doors in 1988,
under the auspices of St Matthias Anglican Church, Centennial Park,
in Sydney, our aim has been to provide the Christian community with
products of a uniformly high standard—both in their biblical faithfulness
and in the quality of the writing and production.

Now known as Matthias Media, we have grown to become a nationwide
provider of user-friendly resources for ministry, with Christians of all sorts
using our Bible studies, books, Briefings, audio cassettes, videos, training
courses—you name it.

For more information about the range of Matthias Media resources,
call us on Freecall **1800 814 360** (or in Sydney 9663-1478),
or fax us on (02) 9662-4289, and we will send you a free catalogue.
Or you can e-mail us at "matmedia@ozemail.com.au".
Or visit our Web site at:

http://www.gospelnet.com.au/matmedia/

Buy direct from us and save

If you order your Matthias Media resources direct from us, you not only
save time and money, you invest in more great resources for the future:

· you save time—we usually despatch our orders within 24 hours
  of receiving them

· you save money—our normal prices are better than other retailers'
  prices (plus if you order in bulk, you'll save even more)

· you help keep us afloat—because we get more from each sale,
  buying from us direct helps us to stay alive in the difficult world
  of publishing.

About Impact Evangelism

In 1990 a group of Christians set up a gospelling agency with one simple aim: to communicate the message of Jesus to as many as possible, as often as possible, as well as possible.

Today, the vision of IMPACT Evangelism remains unchanged. Well-known speaker and author Kim Hawtrey works year-round in partnership with scores of churches, specialising in creative gospel outreach from a reformed, Biblical perspective.

IMPACT also runs training sessions with local churches to equip believers to share their faith, and produces evangelistic resources including books, tapes and tracts.

To receive the 'IMPACT Bulletin', a free quarterly newsletter, or to make general enquiries, telephone IMPACT on **(02) 9982 4092,** send a fax on (02) 9982 4530, or email to "partners@impact.au.nu".

IMPACT Evangelism
GPO Box 1415
Sydney NSW 2001
Australia

www.impact.au.nu

Also available from IMPACT Evangelism

Christianity: a pocket guide by Kim Hawtrey. A brief, user-friendly introduction to the Christian message.